UGANDAN ASIANS IN GREAT BRITAIN

Forced Migration and Social Absorption

UGANDAN ASIANS IN GREAT BRITAIN

FORCED MIGRATION AND SOCIAL ABSORPTION

WILLIAM G. KUEPPER
G. LYNNE LACKEY
E. NELSON SWINERTON

CROOM HELM LONDON

First Published 1975
© 1975 William G. Kuepper, E. Lynne Lackey, E. Nelson Swinerton

Croom Helm Ltd, 2-10 St Johns Road, London SW11

ISBN 0-85664-267-3

Printed by Biddles of Guildford and bound in Great Britain
by Redwood Burn Ltd, Trowbridge and Esher
Typeset by Red Lion Setters, Holborn, London

CONTENTS

Preface and Acknowledgements

In August 1972 the first Asian expellees from Uganda began arriving at London's Heathrow Airport. Within three months over 28,000 were to immigrate to Great Britain. The summary nature of President Idi Amin's expulsion order with its ninety-day exit deadline necessitated an immediate response from researchers interested in initiating a research project to systematically observe the reception and relocation of Ugandan Asians in Great Britain. Our interdisciplinary team, consisting of a geographer, a political scientist and a sociologist, conducted research in Britain during late 1972 and early 1973 on the expelled Ugandan Asian population. Unfortunately, because of complications of time, organisation and need for immediate funding, crisis research is rarely undertaken. The 1956 Hungarian exodus and the Cuban refugee movement in the early sixties, for example, have left largely unrecorded the personal and societal consequences of migration under aggravated circumstances. We believed that an attempt should be made to better understand some of the dynamics of forced migrant transition from one country and culture to another.

Who are the Ugandan Asians? Where did they originally come from, and why were they now forced to leave Uganda? What are their prospects for a new life? Can they be absorbed into British society? From the receiving society's point of view, we asked, how do governments at the national and local levels respond to the sudden influx of thousands of refugees? Would baseline data on governments and societal responses be useful in directing reception of forced migrant populations under similar circumstances in the future? These were some of the many questions that came to mind during the fall of 1972 as we watched from our American vantage point as plane load upon plane load of British Asians were airlifted from Uganda, unlikely ever to return 'home.'

Media reports of Asians being stripped of business, personal possessions and life savings, and harassed en route to the airport added to the concern over the Asians' plight. Noticeable, also were reports of a wary British public reluctant to accept another wave of 'coloured' immigrants on their 'tiny island.' The fact that the British were creating the Uganda Resettlement Board to handle immigrant arrival and relocation, introduced the possibility of studying an organized response to forced migration. Most importantly, the project offered the opportunity to trace the initial stage of forced migrant absorption and provided baseline data for future longitudinal analysis of the absorption process.

1

Released time was provided by the University of Wisconsin-Green Bay to enable us to go to Great Britain. For this support we are grateful. On the other side of the Atlantic, we were moved by the warm reception, encouragement and support by all with whom we had the opportunity to work throughout our stay in Great Britain. Researchers could not ask for better cooperation, assistance and helpful advice.

We wish to acknowledge the assistance of Sir Charles Cunningham and Thomas Critchley and the staff of the Uganda Resettlement Board; Dr Alan Little of the Community Relations Council; John Lyttle of the Race Relations Board; Hannah Stanton and the Co-ordinating Committee for the Welfare of Evacuees from Uganda; Ian McGarry, Leader of the Council of the Borough of Wandsworth, and colleagues; and especially, Charles Boxer and Urmila Patel of the Wandsworth Council for Community Relations; and Terry Holland of the Slough Council for Community Relations. To the many others who aided and encouraged our research, we also extend our heartfelt appreciation.

Most of all, though, we have a debt to the Ugandan Asians in Wandsworth and Slough, who with hospitality and understanding, gave their time and provided the information upon which this study is based.

For her efforts and care in preparation of the manuscript and the many other ways that she helped us, we thank Diane Morey.

We salute our family and friends who offered encouragement and support throughout the project.

William G. Kuepper
G. Lynne Lackey
E. Nelson Swinerton

1. THE UGANDAN ASIAN CRISIS IN PERSPECTIVE

On August 4, 1972 President Idi Amin of Uganda ordered the expulsion of all British Asians from that East African nation. Addressing the officers and men of the Airborne Regiment in Torroro, General Amin declared that Uganda would ask Britain to assume responsibility for all Ugandan Asians holding British passports. The Asians, he contended, were 'sabotaging the economy of the country.'

These Asians were neither a small nor an insignificant minority; they were the acknowledged mainstay of commercial Uganda. Their Ugandan heritage was lengthy, and many could trace their ancestry in East Africa back through several generations. Over this considerable time period, some had indeed amassed impressive holdings. And deliberately or not, all of these Asians had played a role in the development of Uganda and East Africa.

What prompted President Amin's sudden determination that the Asians were an intolerable element in Ugandan society? No singular appraisal alone is adequate, nor can the reasons behind the move necessarily be logically deduced. Was the African leader as ruthless and compulsive as he appeared to much of the outside world? Had the Asians stirred resentment by exploiting the African nation and natives to attain their prominent economic status? Some observers reported that the President's power was on the wane in certain national sectors; thus a number of critics viewed the expulsion as an attempt to revive support through dramatic, and supposedly popular, political action. Possibly another factor frustrating to the General was that, under the quotas Britain had applied to immigration, it would take ten more years to rid Uganda legally of the noncitizen Asians. Whatever the motives, and whether or not they are ever clearly deciphered, the crisis for the Asian minority and for the nations called upon to receive Asian immigrants, had been precipitated.

Precisely which Asians were to be affected by the edict was not immediately clear. The President seemed primarily concerned with alien Asians, particularly those holding British passports. On the other hand, he had a history of making no distinction between citizen and non-citizen Asians; he initially referred to the disquieting figure of 80,000 Asians to be removed, a reasonably good estimate of the total number of Asians in Uganda.

General Amin had set into motion an example of the phenomenon known as forced migration; the Asians assumed the unenviable status of

3

nonvolitional migrants. What then were their prospects? How might they go about the necessary process of adjusting to a new society? And how might another nation react to the influx of this refugee population? Would the Asians, like migrants before them, experience a reduction and narrowing of the social base in which they lived and performed? Could they construct in another nation, namely Britain, a new community of interaction and identity?

This volume examines the Ugandan Asians' early months in Britain; it analyses the initial outlook and response of a forced migrant population as well as the reception of a society hosting the expelled people. No final or conclusive statements about the fate of the Asians in Britain or about their impact on British society can be made from these preliminary observations. Yet, it is valuable to record and assess the contraction and subsequent re-expansion of the migrants' social fields and with the passage of time to trace the expellees' journey through stages in the process of social absorption.

The Emerging Crisis

As news of Amin's announcement spread throughout Uganda and to the rest of the world, three questions repeatedly arose: (1) was the President serious?; (2) if he were, which Asians were affected by the expulsion decree?; and (3) what sort of deadline would consequently be imposed on their departure? Some answers were not long in coming. Amin was serious indeed. Within twenty-four hours, the President had made it clear that he would not rescind his order for the Asian departure and that his demands would have to be fulfilled within three months. Perhaps more than any other aspect of the expulsion, the three-month deadline caused serious concern.

Amin's announcement caught Britain in the midst of a controversy over queue-jumping British Asians who were trying to get into the United Kingdom before they could obtain the proper entry vouchers. The British Government was firmly resisting appeals to further liberalise immigration controls as they applied to British Asians. The number of entry vouchers reserved for British Asians had been doubled from 1,500 to 3,000 per year in 1971 to reduce the long wait of Asian heads-of-households in East Africa to enter Britain. Despite the effects this change had in reducing waiting periods, deteriorating conditions for the Asians in East Africa caused some to jump the queue and attempt to enter Britain before they were legally permitted.

While waiting for official word from General Amin regarding the expulsion of the Asians, the British Government staunchly refused appeals for a change in immigration controls to allow more British Asians entrance into the United Kingdom. For a time, perhaps, Britain felt such resistance would strengthen its position against Amin's flagrant abuse of international norms of behaviour.

But attempts at immigration violations continued. Next in the long line of the impatient were eighteen Kenyan Asians who had arrived in Manchester without proper entry vouchers. They too were turned away. In a statement on 6 August, Mr David Lane, Under Secretary of State, Home Office, emphasised the Government's stand against any further increase in the number of vouchers issued to East African Asians.

Unhappy with the tone of the initial British response, and sensing the discontent created in Britain as well as the popular support arising in Uganda as a result of the announcement, Amin warmed to the task. Earlier he had bitterly attacked Asian and British entrepreneurs, stating that the Asians 'milked the cow, but did not feed it to yield more milk.'[1] Then the General, speaking on International Cooperative Day, accused the Asians of not reinvesting in Uganda and of preventing African businessmen from learning the Asians' skills. 'It must be clearly understood as a guiding principle,' he continued, 'that Uganda's economy must remain under the control of the citizens of Uganda.'[2] Amin paid tribute to the impact of cooperatives on Africanisation and general development of the economy. He repeated his charges of economic sabotage and remained in no mood to change his mind about expelling the Asians.

The timing of the announcement remains a puzzle. It may have resulted from Amin's uneasiness at recent British immigration action. It is possible he feared a reduction in the British Asian immigration quota allotted to East Africa. Some suggest that he made the move as a smokescreen to hide conditions in a deteriorating economy. None of these seems a thorough argument.

A week passed before Great Britain came to terms with the fact that Amin meant what he said and that the November deadline was real. To keep watch over the situation, the Government created a standing committee of ministers and officials. Mr Robert Carr, the Home Secretary and Leader of the House, said on the floor of Parliament that the Government was beginning intense diplomatic activity 'to try to ward off this threatened inhumane treatment of many thousands of Asians, the majority of whom are United Kingdom passport holders.'[3]

In Uganda, a meeting between President Amin, the British and Indian High Commissioners, the Pakistani Ambassador, and leaders of the Asian community only served to reaffirm Amin's rigid position. He reiterated the ninety-day limit condition of his order and confirmed the fact that Asians were to make their own arrangements to leave prior to the deadline. An Amin broadcast discounted the effects of possible withdrawal of British aid. A *Times* correspondent reported the following reaction by Amin to the British request to negotiate: 'This is British imperialism. I am not going to listen to imperialist advice that we should continue to have foreigners control the economy.'4 Announcements of a Ugandan military aid mission to Moscow, and revocation of all entry permits and certificates of residence which had been granted to noncitizen Asians, helped to convince the British Government of the gravity of the situation. Mr Geoffrey Rippon was dispatched as the official envoy from Her Majesty's Government to meet with President Amin and to request reconsideration of the expulsion order.

After many futile attempts, General Amin and Mr Rippon got together on August 16. Later, at a Kampala press conference with General Amin in attendance, Mr Rippon reported that he had been unable to change the President's mind. Britain was preparing to handle the mass exodus of Asians from Uganda. Asked how he thought the British people would react to the influx of 50,000 new immigrants, Mr Rippon replied:

> The real difficulty is in absorbing large numbers of people in a short period of time. But I think the British public accepts that when people have been given United Kingdom passports as a matter of history, and have been given assurances by successive British Governments, that they will honour them if they are expelled and those assurances must be fulfilled.5

He repeated the Government's position upon returning to London. He told a press conference after meeting with Prime Minister Heath, Home Secretary Carr, and Minister of State at the Foreign Office Godber that the Uganda Government also had a responsibility: 'This is a human problem,' he said, 'you cannot treat human beings like cattle. The Asians should be entitled to sell their property and to take their money out of the country.'6 Plans to organise Britain's response were finalised upon Mr Rippon's return. The first step would be to determine the extent to which other countries might help ease the burden by offering to accept refugees. The logistics of moving thousands upon thousands from Uganda to a new home in the British Isles, and hopefully elsewhere, should have generated immediate response by Governments throughout the world.

World Reaction

World reaction to General Amin's expulsion order was, as would be expected, one of shock and dismay. The action was condemned by most countries. But official judgements and remonstrations aside, the pragmatic issue of Asian resettlement demanded attention and response. The Commonwealth nations might have been expected to share the burden of receiving those forced to migrate from Uganda. However, the Government of Canada was the only country to come forward quickly to offer accommodation, and such hospitality was extended exclusively to 'qualified' Asians. Most of the remainder of the Commonwealth countries were reluctant to make a commitment until the full dimensions of the problem were known. Dr Forbes, the Australian Minister for Immigration, speaking in his Parliament on August 22, maintained that the Government should not accede to the British request for cooperation in accepting the Ugandan expellees. Australia would take only such persons as could be 'integrated' into Australian society, meaning, in essence, persons with Anglo-Saxon physical features, who possessed designated skills or professional qualifications. Applications for landed immigrant status from Asians in Uganda would be considered on 'individual merit.' The New Zealand Prime Minister was quick to call on Commonwealth countries to reproach General Amin for his policy on Asians, but he was reluctant to indicate whether New Zealand was prepared to receive any of the expellees. Even the Government of India contended that all Asians in East Africa holding British passports were Britain's responsibility.

Much of the world was interested in the reaction of Uganda's neighbours – Tanzania, Kenya and Zambia. Each has a sizeable Asian minority, and each is under pressure to increase Black control of the economy. President Nyerere of Tanzania attacked Amin's policy, stating, 'Every racialist in the world is an animal of some kind or another, and all are kinds which have no future. Eventually, they will become extinct.'[7] The condemnation followed the General's inclusion of Asians who were Ugandan citizens in his expulsion order. In the same speech, the Tanzanian leader also took Britain to task for its policy toward Asians. 'Citizens must be accepted without discrimination,'[8] he contended. President Kaunda of Zambia called the expulsion 'terrible, horrible, abominable and shameful.' 'Wherever there was human suffering,' said Kaunda, 'it gave no cause for rejoicing. Seeds of the trouble had been sown before Uganda's independence when the Asians were encouraged to become British citizens, but it was not right to commit another wrong because of Britain's treatment many years ago.'[9] President Amin's Information Ministry retorted the following day: 'Dr Kaunda is an imperialist agent and a black sheep among African leaders.'[10]

In Kenya, President Kenyatta maintained a stern silence, but Vice-President Daniel Arap Moi suggested that the Kenyan policy toward Africanisation would proceed in an orderly fashion without prejudicing the rights of citizens. However, Moi additionally proclaimed that the border between his nation and Uganda would be sealed to prevent migration of Ugandan Asians into Kenya. 'Kenya is not a dumping ground for citizens of other countries,'[11] he said. Later, Mr Martin Shikuhu, Kenya's Minister of Home Affairs, went a step further, calling General Amin's decree a 'timely and wise decision to give the Ugandans the right to control their economy.' He cautioned Kenyan residents without citizenship that they too would have to leave 'unless they stopped sabotaging Kenya's economy and sending money abroad.'[12] The only African leader to offer the General any tangible sign of support was President Bokassa of the Central African Republic; he relayed a gift of commando uniforms to Amin.

The international press took a dim view of Amin's actions. The Nigerian newspaper *Renaissance* commented, 'President Idi Amin of Uganda should rescind his decision to expel all Asians with British passports in the interest of the Black race.'[13] The Frankfurt daily newspaper, *Frankfurter Allgemeine Zeitung*, said:

> The troubles of the expelled 'Jews of Africa' and Britain's trouble makes it difficult for us to consider only our own anxieties and to disregard the troubles of others as if unconcerned; especially for us Germans who have experienced racialism itself, we who anyway take in foreign workers such as Algerians and Moroccans. In this situation, can we really refuse to shoulder a sizeable part of the burden?[14]

The *Times* of India criticised the Indian Government for its mild response to the plight of Ugandan Asians. The paper also found '. . . wholly inadequate the provisions the Ugandan Government has made for the repatriation of the assets of Asians who are being expelled from the country.'[15] *The New York Times*, addressing the question of India's 'cool response,' posited that New Delhi's desire to promote Afro-Asian solidarity made it less willing to recognise the problem, 'preferring the fiction that the term racism applies only to 'whites' discriminating against coloured people.'[16] *The New York Times* was, however, quick to point out that racism may have more than a single source: 'One mitigating factor behind President Amin's expulsion order has been the failure of most Indian and Pakistani migrants over several generations to integrate with the African community.'[17] An editorial in the London *Times*, not unexpectedly given the forecast migrant invasion of Britain, called on the United Nations to summon a conference to consider appropriate action. 'There is no single country,' argued the *Times* ' — except of course defaulting Uganda — that can or should be saddled with responsibility for the refugees. All aspects of their resettlement must be worked out through the cooperation of a great many governments.'[18]

Whether or not all Asians, citizens as well as noncitizens, would be expelled was a major question in the world press. Some could understand the General's asking noncitizens to leave, but most newspapers emphasised that by asking all citizens of Asian heritage to leave, Amin was cutting at the fabric of international order. Later, this pressure would finally help convince the General to modify his expulsion order to exclude Asians with valid Ugandan citizenship.

Refugees in the Modern World

Ugandan Asians are not alone in their experience of expulsion. Since 1945 alone, over 45 million persons have been denied residence in their homelands for a variety of social and political reasons;[19] and many of these persons became forced migrants.

Contributing to this number of uprooted persons were those hundreds of thousands involved in the mass Hindu-Moslem population exchange initiated in 1947, the many thousands displaced by territorial exchanges related to the varying fortunes of the Third Reich, 250,000 Indonesian Dutch repatriated to Holland, and thousands of Bulgarian Turks returning to western Turkey in the early 'fifties. In addition, nearly 4 million North Koreans had no place to call home at the end of the Korean War, and hundreds of thousands of Vietnamese have been left homeless as the consequence of forty years of warfare. These are but a few examples.

From a somewhat earlier era come two clear-cut examples of persons displaced as a consequence of forced migration. The slave trade, in which unknown millions were physically removed from Africa and transferred to the Americas, is attributed with producing one of history's largest intercontinental migrations. In North America, many native Americans — and again their numbers will never be known — were driven and transported from their homelands to foreign territories and reservations. The Cherokees' 'Trail of Tears' leading west from North Carolina is a poignant example. The inhumane policy of establishing reserves for 'natives' flourishes yet in this century as South Africa continues to rationalise its transfer of the African population to the Homelands. A few specific examples of recent crisis migrations stimulate speculation as to how groups which vary in patterns of exodus and conditions to which they fled, might consequently vary in their modes and rates of social adaptation in the new settings. The Cubans, the Hungarians and the South Sudanese provide three illuminating cases.

Cuban Refugees

In the early 'sixties, thousands fled Cuba's communist government. At one point in the fall of 1962, 1,700 refugees were swarming into Florida every week; 500,000 in all would reach U.S. shores. Many came on a parole status, some with no visas, and many were technically listed as tourists. The U.S. Department of Health, Education and Welfare established the Cuban Refugee Emergency Center and provided basic relief funds to the refugees. The magnitude of the problem did not become apparent at first due to the fact that Miami's 50,000 permanent Cuban residents helped to absorb the first several waves of refugees. Gradually, however, the resources of the Greater Miami area became strained in terms of housing, employment and school facilities. The mass of refugees who were allowed to take with them from Cuba only the equivalent of $5, required considerable assistance to move out of the Miami area to urban centres across the United States.

Unlike the Asians who left virtually all their possessions in Uganda and had little hope of returning, most of the Cubans anticipated a return home as soon as the Castro regime failed. But the dictator's government flourished, and residence on the mainland developed into a necessary and, for most, a tolerable permanency. The opportunity to settle with Cubans in New York, Los Angeles, Chicago and other major cities helped ease adjustment to the United States. Like the Ugandan Asians who found Asian neighbourhoods in the London boroughs and in other metropolitan areas of Great Britain, the Cubans were able to gain a foothold in their new society through the help of government agencies, local voluntary organisations, relatives and friends.

Hungarian Exodus

The Hungarian refugees from the October 1956 insurrection are normally described as typical political refugees. For most of the 170,000 Hungarians who participated in the mass migration, it was to be a permanent exodus from their homeland. Only several thousand returned home in the first six-month period following the revolution. Twenty-seven countries and a host of international organisations worked to provide emergency relief action. Over 100,000 persons were evacuated from their first destination, Austria, immediately across the border from Hungary. France, Israel, Britain, the United States, Canada and Yugoslavia accepted considerable numbers of the refugees. In the United States, as one example, emergency refugee camps were established at places like Camp Kilmer, New Jersey to process the Hungarians to new jobs and homes across the country. Local communities organised committees to welcome families and to help the bewildered newcomers begin life again.

These Hungarians, unlike many of the Ugandan Asians and the Cubans, did not find themselves moving into ethnic neighbourhoods populated with relatives or family friends. For most, both their exodus and their final destination were functions of chance and were unrelated to an existing social network. Over 5,000 of the 21,000 who migrated to Britain during the first six months after the insurrection went on to Canada. They were replaced in Britain by a comparable number from Austrian camps. One of the major differences in the Hungarian resettlement in Europe and North America, as compared to the Ugandan Asian resettlement under examination, is the issue of race. While absence of a colour barrier has hastened the Hungarian group's absorption into these societies, the Asians' ready identifiability by physical characteristics will inevitably impede their acceptance.

The Southern Sudanese

Amin's move against the Asians in his country is only part of a larger picture of nonvolitional migration of refugees across the African continent. By early 1973, the United Nations had identified at least 1 million refugees on that continent. About half of these had fled colonial masters, but some 500,000 of them had been displaced by independent African governments. Counted in the UN's total are thousands of Sudanese refugees who, in response to religious and racial oppression, fled over a seventeen-year period to the neighbouring countries of Uganda, Zaire, Ethiopia, and the Central African Republic.

Aided by the United Nations' agencies, or more typically by kin and friends, almost all of the Sudanese migrants settled in rural areas. They brought with them basic agrarian skills that served them well under conditions of their relocation. Many also displayed a willingness to make adjustments necessary to their new life. But the asylum countries were seldom in a position to harness this flexibility, nor were they able to effectively utilise the skills of the small minority of better educated Sudanese who became especially frustrated with their new existence.

How did the Sudanese immigrants fare after leaving their homeland? Clearly, the answer is mixed. Some did badly, but many seemed to begin carving out a satisfactory existence for themselves with only modest changes in lifestyle. However, permanency did not characterise this resettlement. One expert on refugees suggested that the flight from war and persecution was but 'a migration in the typical African tradition,' and when things began to change in the Sudan, the Sudanese began '. . . migrating home again.'[20]

Adaptation of the Ugandan Asians

Long before the expelled Ugandans arrived in Britain in 1972, an Asian community had established itself as part of the increasingly heterogeneous population of the British Isles. Indians and Pakistanis, including

11

the East African Asians, constitute a visible South Asian ethnic group which in order of population size, ranks fourth among minorities in England and Wales. The Irish (by far the largest minority), West Indians and the Jews (the latter two groups with numbers only slightly greater than the Asians) rank ahead of them.[21] Estimates based on census enumeration put the combined Indian-Pakistani population at 350,000,[22] or at one per cent of the base population.

Familiar ethnic enclaves provided by the Asians resident in Britain are an attractive and protective feature of British society for the Ugandan Asians. Likewise, the native Britons, while far from unanimous in their welcoming of the expellees, are acquainted with an Asian populace and perhaps less inclined to view the newcomers as peculiar or threatening. But do these factors provide assurance of the Ugandan Asians' successful transition into British society?

The African experience of the Ugandan Asians must be considered in assessing their social prospects in Britain. What were their relationships to the native African community and to the former colonial regime? The social background attributes which the immigrants bring with them to Britain must be in part, a consequence of the involvement of the Asian community in British Africa. For example, do the styles of life and levels of education of the immigrants approximate those of the Britishers among whom they will now live?

The receptivity of the national and local communities will affect Asian adjustment. Has the machinery of resettlement been effective? Are political and economic circumstances amenable to the inward migration of an Asian population? Important characteristics of the migration, migrants and the host society can all be predicted to significantly influence this adaptation process.

A tool useful in examining the state of the Asians' adjustment following their initial period of residence in Great Britain is the social field model. The social field is composed of that complex of roles and interaction patterns played out by any given individual, or on a larger scale, by any group of individuals related by role assignments and shared interaction.

An attribute of the social field particularly pertinent to the study of migration is its tendency to expand as the level of individual or group integration into a society increases. In the case of the migrant, and especially the forced migrant, there is, as the person vacates roles in many formal and informal groups, a consequent sharp contraction of the social field. The multiplicity of roles the Asians played in the Ugandan environment — roles such as brother, husband, employee, friend, affiliate of various secondary groups, etc. — may, for example, have been suddenly reduced to but a few. Because all roles are defined only in relationship to other roles, the disbanding of a community,

12

whether it be an Asian district of Kampala or Jinja, or the very movement away from a homeland, necessarily effects a reduction in role activities. Furthermore, this same contraction may have occurred in terms of the Ugandan Asians' statuses, i.e. their social positions. Hierarchies are by definition the consequence of persons ranking themselves in relation to others. It would be expected that many, if not most, such positions held by the Ugandan Asians would disappear with exodus from a community or with the dissolution of the community itself. If in fact the Asians' exodus had sharply reduced their social field — the breadth and structure of the interactional and institutional milieu around which their lives were shaped — the rate of movement toward absorption would depend in large measure on their ability to construct a new field in Britain. By examining the emergence of this social field, it is possible to assess the immigrants' progress toward adaptation to British society.

Viewing adaptation more closely, specific stages or phases in the reconstruction of the field can be delineated. Factors affecting the extension of social participation and orientation beyond small primary groups to the larger society will also affect the rate at which the immigrant group passes through the phases of the adaptive cycle. Taking into consideration perspectives of those who have examined such assimilative processes,[23] an inclusive and useful description of the cycle would be the following: acceptance, acculturation and absorption.

Acceptance

The first stage — acceptance — refers to the level of tolerance migrants bring to, or develop for, the new situation. Are the Ugandan Asians willing to accept the host society as their home? Have they brought or cultivated a sense of commitment to the society? Has, for example, their historical familiarity with the British bred a respect for Anglo-Saxon traditions and ways of life? Were their colonial encounters with the Britons such to promote tolerance of present British society and to foster a desire to become an active participant in the host society? Acceptance prepares the way by assuring the motivation for entry into the following two stages. Acceptance is the requisite 'set' for learning and participating in new social patterns. It infers a willingness to conform to significant social norms and dictates of the new society.

Acculturation

The process of acquiring the culture and life ways of a society, and which typically involves adopting a variety of new behavioural forms, is generally referred to as acculturation. This new behaviour may include attaining language skills; acquiring and adhering to the folk-ways, norms and values of the host society; and recognising and acting out modified or new role expectations. How acculturated to English traditions are the Asians, and do they respect the British social heritage enough to embrace major portions of it readily? The greater the overlap of learned values, attitudes and life ways between the Ugandan Asians and the British, the more quickly the Asians will be able to participate in host institutions. Likewise, to the extent that the Asian refugees share cultural features of the new society, there will be among the British a greater inclination toward tolerance and acceptance of the forced migrants. Absolute acculturation, or the adherence to all social and cultural norms of the host society, is not, however, requisite to attaining stage three — absorption.

Absorption

Participation in the major institutions of society constitutes social absorption. Earning wages through reputable employment is, for example, one link to the economic institution, while voting and party affiliation indicate ties to the political institution. To attain this degree of social integration, there is a minimal level of acculturation which groups like the Ugandan Asians must achieve. Certain types of information or knowledge — language is a good example — are essential to social participation. Acculturation, beyond the rudimentary level, then, may continue while absorption is taking place and even after it has occurred. For the Ugandan Asians, complete acculturation need, in fact, never take place; acquisition of those traits necessary for participation in the host British society does not require that the Asians abandon all social forms which differ from those of the dominant society.

It is, of course, the recipient society that ultimately controls the extent and rate of migrant absorption. Prejudice and discriminatory behaviour directed toward the newcomers will retard and can prohibit social participation. In order to be discriminated against, a group must be identifiable; consequently, the more unique or distinguishing characteristics a group has, the more likely it is to be singled out for special or discriminatory treatment. As the Asians are characterised by both cultural and physical traits differing from the larger host community, the issue becomes one of the degree to which these distinctions will affect absorption.

The following attributes and behaviour, to briefly summarise, would then typify migrants at each of the various levels of social field expansion. Acceptance could be exemplified by the Asian eager to acquire skills and social knowledge characteristic of a new society. A Ugandan Asian would be acculturated when he affects the critical values, customs and habits native to his area of settlement, and absorption could be distinguished when he has structured his behaviour,

14

his life, around activities sponsored and condoned by the major British social institutions.

Forms of Migration and Social Absorption

Important to emphasise is the fact that the form of migration itself can be expected to influence adaptation. Volitional migration, it is speculated, results in more rapid migrant adjustment than does non-volitional migration. The extent to which forced migration puts the Ugandan Asians at a disadvantage in terms of social adaptation is a major concern of this study. The voluntary migrant has in all probability advanced well into the acceptance stage of adaptation prior to migration. He has opted to move to a society whose life ways and social opportunities seem attractive. By contrast, the nonvolitional migrant typically begins the cycle on arrival in his new home state. During the first six months of transition to British society, the period under investigation in this book, the Ugandan Asians could be expected to display characteristics of a migrant group embarking on the initial phase of adaptation. Logically and essentially, the focus of this study is on that primary phase of the cycle.

Unlike the volitional migrant who will often select a nation for settlement on the basis of perceived ease of absorption, the forced migrant may find himself relocated in very unfamiliar, and from his perspective, perhaps undesirable, surroundings. The volitional migrant often has the opportunity to weigh the advantages and disadvantages of departure; he is typically convinced that his action is the most favourable of those available to him. Vacillating attitudes regarding resettlement and uncertain prospects in a new society may cause the forced migrant, in this case the Ugandan Asians, to undergo a protracted period of adjustment.

The size of the migrant population and the rapidity with which, to use the social ecologists' terminology, it 'invades' a society also influences its reception and likelihood of quick acceptance by that society. The larger the proportion of immigrants to natives, or the equally important perception of influx size, the more hostile the reaction to the newcomers is likely to be. Also, if movement into a nation occurs very quickly, as with the Asians in a ninety-day period, the migrant group will be perceived by the host society as more threatening than if arrivals are in smaller segments dispersed through time. Forced migration almost inevitably produces a rapid influx of persons into receiving societies. From a functional point of view, it is also typically easier for a society to accommodate and absorb small groups of people over a longer period than it is to accept that same number of people emigrating over a shorter time span. The mixed

British perception and reception of the forced migrant Asian is an interesting case for examination.

In spite of its relatively common occurrence, forced migration has been largely overlooked by researchers. In fact, one discovers that as the degree of choice involved in the movement declines, so does the body of information about the event. The reasons for this deficiency are not without justification. Migration of this sort frequently occurs with little or no forewarning; not only are other nations typically unprepared to cope with population influxes spawned by such crises, but also, in most cases, students concerned with the effects of such phenomena are equally unprepared to systematically observe and record the events. Much of the literature on forced migration which does exist consists of after-the-fact and often necessarily speculative statements about events, reactions and results of that which had transpired. Such reports are not without merit. They are, however, far from a desirable statement of actual occurrences, far from a consideration of concurrently observed effects of and responses to forced migration.[24]

For readily acknowledged theoretical reasons, understanding the processes and effects of forced migration is desirable. The more aspects and attributes of migration that are examined, the closer students of the field are to formulation of explanatory and prognostic theory. Other motivations for examining involuntary migration are also significant. Chief among these is the goal of eventually understanding reactions to such events sufficiently well to reduce the trauma and enhance the readjustment of individuals and groups uprooted by such crises. The problems of refugees are hardly modern or rare, yet individual anxieties and predispositions associated with that status, and pressures exerted on societies which inherit such populations, are little understood. Potentially, research on the topic can, on the humanitarian level, both promote comprehension of the process and reduce problems associated with it.

Notes

1. *Uganda Argus,* August 1, 1972.
2. *Ibid.,* August 7, 1972.
3. The *Times*, August 10, 1972.
4. *Ibid.,* August 11, 1972.
5. *Ibid.,* August 16, 1972.
6. *Ibid.,* August 17, 1972.
7. *Ibid.,* August 15, 1972.
8. *Ibid.,* August 15, 1972.
9. *Ibid.,* September 7, 1972.
10. *Ibid.,* September 8, 1972.
11. *Ibid.,* August 9, 1972.

12. *Ibid.*, August 22, 1972.
13. *Ibid.*, August 8, 1972.
14. *Ibid.*, August 19, 1972.
15. *Ibid.*, September 6, 1972.
16. *Ibid.*, September 29, 1972.
17. *Ibid.*
18. *Ibid.*, August 21, 1972.
19. United Nations, *Refugee Report*, 1969.
20. As quoted in Peter Robbs, 'The Return of the Refugees,' *Africa Report*, November-December 1972, p.17.
21. Ernest Krausz, *Ethnic Minorities in Britain* (London, 1972), p.36.
22. See E.J.B. Rose, *Colour and Citizenship* (London, 1969), Appendix, Table III, iv, 'Adjustment of Census Estimates by Reference to Net Arrivals.'
23. The following are representative and important examples of theory pertaining to adaptation stages among migrants and/or minorities: S.N. Eisenstadt, *The Absorption of Immigrants*; Milton M. Gordon, *Assimilation in American Life*; R.E. Park and E.W. Burgess, *Introduction to the Science of Sociology* (the 'race relations cycle'); and R. Taft, *From Stranger to Citizen.*
24. Notable exceptions to the general inadequacy include studies of Indians and Pakistanis displaced when British India was partitioned in 1947, and William Peterson's (see, for example, 'A General Typology of Migration,' *American Sociological Review* [June 1958], pp. 256-266) attempts to acquaint social scientists with distinctions between types of migration and implications of such distinctions.

2. THE EAST AFRICAN HERITAGE

The arrival in Britain of nearly 28,000 Ugandan Asians during sixty days in September, October and November of 1972 represented a sharp intensification of a continuing movement of people from East Africa* to the United Kingdom. The immigration to Great Britain of large numbers of Commonwealth citizens, including many from the Indian subcontinent, had been substantial for over two decades. But in recent years, most of the British Asians arriving in the United Kingdom had spent much, if not all, of their lives in East Africa. From where did they originally come? Why were they in East Africa, and what roles did they play? To what degree were Asian communities developed there, and to what extent were the Asians absorbed into Ugandan society? Why did their social field, expanding over several decades, suddenly collapse? Would the Asians' experience in East Africa make absorption into British society an easier or a more difficult task? This chapter, reviewing the Asians' background in Uganda, seeks to answer these questions.

⋅ All the Ugandan Asians were migrants or descendants of recent migrants to Africa. Those not born in East Africa made the journey from India voluntarily. Contrary to popular belief, only a small portion of the Ugandan Asians traced their ancestry to migrant indentured labourers. None came under any government scheme for increasing the non-African population. None except the recruits for the construction of the Uganda Railway were assisted financially by either the governments of India or of East Africa. The migration of most Indians to East Africa thus was not only volitional, but also unofficial and spontaneous. In many cases, it was encouraged by friends or relatives already established in East Africa. Few Africans possessed, at that time, the crafts and skills so badly needed in the expanding East African economic sphere. The opportunities for the Indians were obvious.

The lure of East Africa was, of course, not the only motive for the emigration from India. During the first half of the twentieth century, Indians were leaving the subcontinent for other parts of the Commonwealth and Empire as well. Crowding, food shortages and

---

* East Africa or British East Africa is used to denote the area encompassing the nations of Kenya, Tanzania and Uganda. Prior to World War I, mainland Tanzania (Tanganyika) was under German colonial rule and was part of what was officially called German East Africa.

unemployment were chronic and at times acute in British India, and these conditions were exacerbated by a rapidly expanding population. The forces acting to encourage out-migration were, if not compelling, at least very strong in parts of the subcontinent.

Most of the twentieth-century Asian immigrants to East Africa came from Kathiawad, Cutch, and particularly Gujerat, areas which produced the early traders. Unlike the indentured railway workers, almost all paid for the trip themselves or arranged financing through relatives or friends – in many cases from among those already in East Africa. The cost of such a voyage was not small, and the very poor, not having access to the necessary funds, seldom had the means to emigrate. The rich, on the other hand, did not have the desire or need to do so.

The migrants came largely from a rural farm or village environment. Few lived far from the port cities which for centuries served the Indian trade with East Africa. Culturally, historically, and economically the bulk of the Indian immigrants to East Africa had far more in common with the early sailors, traders and moneylenders than they did with the indentured railway workers.

The colonial environment into which the Asian migrants were moving provided both opportunities for and constraints upon their economic, political and social activities. While some officials clearly were less enthusiastic than others about immigration from India, there was a *de facto* recognition in British East Africa of the importance of Asians to the economic development of the area. The Asians' economic role was to provide for themselves whatever degree of acceptance they achieved in the colonial society. Their economic status also was ultimately to be the major source of contention between the Asian immigrants and the indigenous Africans.[1]

To better understand the nature of their role in Uganda, their place in the Ugandan society, and the attitude which developed toward them, an analysis of the Asians' early involvement along the East Africa coast is necessary.

Early Days in East Africa

One of the most important occurrences in the history of East Africa, and certainly the best known in the history of Asians in that region, was the construction of the Uganda Railway initiated at the end of the nineteenth century. Conceived as a means (1) to aid in administration and control of new British holdings in the East Africa interior and (2) to encourage the economic development of these regions, the railway was built substantially by Indian indentured workers. Crucial, widely acclaimed, and well known as was the importation of coolie labour for the railroad, it represented neither the initiation of important Asian contact with the area, nor as mentioned above, was it to provide the bulk of the region's Asian population. The story of Asians in East Africa began much earlier. Indeed, by the time the railroad workers arrived, attitudes of mistrust and envy of the East African Asian community were already widespread.

For centuries the merchants of Western India had been doing business along the East African coast. The coast, so effectively shielded from European adventurers by distance and desert, was open to the sailors of the Arabian Sea for two thousand years. Riding the same seasonal reversal of winds which powered the trade routes between the Persian Gulf and Western India, the Indian, Arab, and Persian sailors and traders made the East African coast a relatively straightforward extension of that lucrative traffic.[2]

For hundreds of years ivory, skins and slaves from East Africa were exchanged for ironware, cloth, beads and spices brought in by the Asian merchants. From the beginning, Indian merchants were an integral part of the trade, living and conducting business in towns the Arabs established. By A.D. 1300, with the trade routes of the Western Indian Ocean controlled by Muslim, Arab and Indian, the coast of East Africa was dotted with perhaps as many as six dozen towns, steadily growing in size and wealth. The merchants were growing richer, the rulers more powerful, and a coastal culture was flourishing.

Then, as the sixteenth century began, Europe intruded on the East African scene 'like an unseasonable monsoon for which the inhabitants were wholly unprepared.'[3] Seeking a route to the Orient and control of the lucrative Indian Ocean trade, the Portuguese reached East Africa and began the business of subjugating the Arab coastal settlements. The Portuguese quickly gained ascendancy in the Western Indian Ocean. This control, attendant political unrest, and the concurrent trade lethargy along the East African coast reduced the incentive for Indian entrepreneurs, but never discouraged them completely.

In the 1800s a renewal of commercial activity along the East African coast was spurred by French interest in obtaining slaves for their agricultural operations on the Ile de France. As the French trade in slaves grew, it encouraged a revival of the ancient Arab traffic in the same commodity. And as in the past, Indians played an important role in financing the Arab trade.

Zanzibar was one of the few coastal towns to profit from the revitalised trade. More and more it became the centre of commercial activity in Eastern Africa. Indian merchants, in response to the increasing importance of Zanzibar, travelled on a regular basis to the island in order to participate in various commercial enterprises, particularly that of financing the trade in slaves.

The modern history of Indian involvement in East Africa began with the reign of Said bin Sultan, the ruler of Muscat. Realising the considerable advantages offered by Zanzibar, Said moved the capital of his domain from the Arabian peninsula to the tropical island. Muscat was the most popular Persian Gulf state for Indian merchants, and many migrated to Zanzibar with Said. With the same type of encouragement they received in Muscat, the traders settled and quickly asserted themselves in all facets of commercial activities. By 1833 one of the Indian firms, Wat Benia, already had acquired the profitable and prestigious post of customs collector for Zanzibar.[4]

The scope of the trade that Said encouraged was not significantly different from that which had been going on for centuries. Two priorities of Said, however, did have profound effects on later events. He encouraged development of Arab caravan routes in the interior; the red flag of the sultan became a familiar sight deep into East Africa. He also opened a large slave market on Zanzibar, expanding that trade at a time when the West African slave trade was already finished.

The Indian community was active in both enterprises. Indian merchants began penetrating into the interior with the Arabs, and Indian merchants financed many of the caravans which were bringing slaves out to the Zanzibar market. By the mid-1860s, over 5,000 Indians lived in the sultan's East African domains, and they controlled almost the entire Zanzibari trade, estimated to have reached over £1½ million per year. Their investments in East Africa were equally impressive, one firm alone having over £400,000 in loans and mortgages.[5] The Indian entrepreneurs were so dominant in the sultan's enterprises that they became, in fact, the 'commercial agents of Arab power.'[6]

The success of the Zanzibar slave trade began to attract the serious attention of the British. East Africa's part in the grand design of British imperialism was related to its strategic location in protecting 'the all-important stakes in India and the East.'[7] But early in the nineteenth century the suppression of the slave trade became a more immediate motive for British involvement in East Africa. In the mid-1900s, the British Consul on Zanzibar attacked the problem by concentrating on the Indian traders. As British subjects, those traders were not legally permitted to participate in any slave trade. But the East African slave trade itself remained legal until 1873, and slavery was not abolished on Zanzibar until 1897. The Indian community found itself, therefore, in a difficult position. A good deal of the tolerance of the Indians, displayed by the Arabs, traditionally resulted from the importance of the Indian merchants in the Zanzibar economy. Their withdrawal from slave trade activities could provide a serious threat to that economy and to their status in Zanzibar.

Destroying slavery on Zanzibar even as late as the 1890s created serious economic difficulties. The Arab owners of the clove plantations, already mortgaged to the hilt with Indian moneylenders, claimed they could not afford to hire labourers even if they would have been inclined to do so. The Asian traders and financiers thus survived the demise of the slave trade in far better shape than did the Arabs. The end of the trade, while a blow to the Arab merchants, had no such negative effect on the Indian traders and moneylenders. The Indians, in fact, 'seized the opportunity afforded them by the abolition of slavery, to oust by loan and foreclosure the ancient Arab trade of which Zanzibar was the centre.'[8] British influence grew and Indian merchants, encouraged to pursue 'legitimate commerce' under the British flag, prospered. The Indian domination of the trade of Zanzibar and thus of Eastern Africa became overwhelming.

During the middle and late 1800s, the Asians' activities as monopolistic merchants, as moneylenders, and as slave traders, were to provide considerable ammunition for those who opposed their dominance of Zanzibar commerce. Crafty, cunning, unscrupulous, dishonest, purveyors of stolen merchandise — these were the comments regarding the Asian merchants and moneylenders. Sir Richard Burton, generally critical of the Indians, referred to the traders as the 'local Jews.'[9]

The Asians of course were accused of financing the slave trade and of being the most active agents in it. It was perfectly predictable that the Indians to some degree would be involved in the traffic of slaves. As customs collectors, merchants and financiers, it was inevitable that they would be participants, if only indirect ones, in one of East Africa's major economic activities. By no means were they alone.

At this same time a different charge was levelled against the Indians on Zanzibar, a charge that was to haunt East African Asians from that day on. They were accused of having no permanent stake in the country, being '. . . mere birds of passage who had no thought of settling in Zanzibar.'[10] The tendency, particularly among the Hindus, of leaving wife and family behind in India in no small way contributed to that impression.

A pattern of criticism was emerging. The Asians were beginning to serve a 'scapegoat' role — a role which was to persist and to grow.[11] Thus, before the first indentured railroad workers arrived, before the first rail was laid, before the bulk of the immigration from the sub-continent began, the Asian community not only attained a major importance in East Africa, it aroused a good deal of suspicion and envy and evoked considerable criticism.

The opposition to Indian involvement in East Africa was by no means a uniformly held one. Many government officials fully recognised the potential value of the Indian to the development of East

Africa. In 1875, Lord Salisbury, Secretary of State for India, went so far as to recommend Indian emigration to East Africa for the purpose of settlement and colonisation. He suggested that both the imperial designs of Britain and humanitarian purposes would be served by sending these 'intelligent and industrious people' to an area climatically well suited to receive them.[12]

The Government's endorsement of Indian involvement, and its concern for the well-being of Indian subjects in East Africa were emphasised in the preamble to the charter of the Imperial British East African Company (IBEA):

> The possession of the British company of the Coast line . . . would be advantageous to the commercial and other interests of our subjects in the Indian Ocean who would otherwise become compelled to reside and trade under the Government or protection of alien powers.

For a brief period in the latter part of the nineteenth century, British designs in East Africa were being formulated and executed by the IBEA. The Company's main objective was to 'prime the pump of legitimate trade.'[13] Financially, the IBEA was a disaster, but its operations in the East African interior had snatched Uganda from Imperial Germany and saved it for Imperial Britain. Before its demise, the IBEA pleaded for a railway to connect Uganda with the East African coast. Arguments raged over the merits of such a line. The issue was not only of a railroad − it also was of British Uganda. Against those who saw the country as a colonial white elephant, Captain Frederick Lugard, IBEA's man in Uganda, hurled the full weight of his increasing prominence. In a letter to the *Times*, he defended it not only as a region to which Europeans could emigrate, but also as a safety valve for the mounting population pressures of British India.[14]

The battles continued, and the fate of Uganda ebbed and flowed, but it finally was to be an imperialists' victory. The British Government accepted the concepts of a protectorate status for Uganda and of a communications link between the protectorate and the East African coast. In 1896, Parliament authorised the Uganda Railway.

Because of the African's inability or unwillingness to provide the skill and labour necessary for the railroad's construction, it was decided to import Indian coolies. The need for Indian workers to build the railroad increased pressure on the Indian Government, which had denied earlier East African requests from both the IBEA and the Germans for indentured labour. When the Indian Government did relent, it did so only on certain important conditions. Among these was the clause that forbade wages of the coolies to be based on productivity. This undoubtedly cost the British both time and money. The most important condition the Indian Government imposed, however, guaranteed that those indentured to work on the railroad be given the right to remain in East Africa at the expiration of their contract.

Some 32,000 indentured artisans and labourers were employed during the six years it took to run the railroad from Mombasa to Kisumu. Due to difficulties of recruiting caused by plague in parts of India, most of the workers were Muslims from the Punjab. The task they faced in building the railroad was difficult, and the toll extracted by the African environment was heavy. Two thousand four hundred and ninety-three of the workers died, and 6,454 were sent home due to illness. Of those who survived their term of service, 16,312 went back to India and 6,724 stayed in East Africa. It is as a result of those 6,700 that a persistent myth arose – most Asians in British East Africa descended from indentured 'coolie' labourers.

The myth served a useful purpose in rationalising certain basic anti-Asian attitudes among the Europeans.[15] Some difficulties, to be sure, arose as a result of the presence of the labourers. Small numbers of time-expired coolies, with no visible means of support, presented the Government with problems, as did over-zealous traders who stepped beyond the geographical constraints placed on their activities.

It seemed of little consequence to the Europeans that some of those who came to work for the railroad company were craftsmen, clerks and engineers. Nor did it matter that those Indians who preceded the railroad workers and those who were to follow were of a higher economic and social status.[16]

The building of the railroad did have far broader implications for the Asian community in East Africa than the adding of 6,700 Indian indentured labourers to its numbers. The railroad acted as the single most important incentive for the Indians to move inland. As the railroad advanced, so too did the vanguard of the institutions of British India: Indian law, Indian administrative practices, Indian currency, and to make it all work, Indian manpower. It was, as Sir Harry Johnston (at that time Commissioner of Uganda) described, '. . . a wedge of India, two miles wide right across East Africa from Mombasa to Victoria Nyanza.'[17]

The growing Asian presence in the interior and the 'officially sponsored immigration' which initiated it, were, along with expanding economic opportunities, the major East Africa factors encouraging further immigration from the subcontinent. The most important result of the presence of the indentured railroad workers in East Africa apart, of course, from the completion of the railroad itself, would seem to be the incentive they, their immigration and their accomplishment provided for those who were to follow.[18]

24

Development of the Asians' Economic Role

The importation of labour for the railroad raised again an issue that initially was a concern of the IBEA. Agricultural development was rightly discerned as a necessity if East Africa were to be self-sufficient. The Company sought to encourage Indian peasants to emigrate to East Africa and to initiate a cash-crop economy. As early as 1891, a scheme was proposed to settle Indian farmers along some of the main rivers in the IBEA domain, but the Indians showed little interest in the undertaking.

Several attempts were made to promote Indian cash cropping in East Africa after the turn of the century, but an unsteady government endorsement of the concept, and a continuing lack of enthusiasm on the part of the Indians in East Africa, caused them to fail. Despite their basically rural background, the bulk of the Indian immigrants, obviously encouraged by the economic success of the petty traders, seemed more inclined toward commerce than agriculture.

An increasingly powerful argument against the encouragement of the Indian peasant was the growing European settler community in East Africa.[19] Proponents of white settlement regarded large portions of both the two main British territories in East Africa (i.e. Uganda and Kenya) as suitable for European agriculture, and viewed the European settler as a far more desirable civilising element than the Indian peasant, trader or merchant, and convinced the Government to restrict Asian land ownership.[20] They saw as their ultimate weapon against the Asians the control of entry from British India, desiring, as Sir Charles Eliot, Protectorate Commissioner, put it, 'to regulate immigration, and open or close the door as seems best.'[21] A petition submitted in 1902 by the settlers supported restrictions on Indian immigration. While it had little chance of influencing British policy and failed to do so, it did contain a charge that was to appear again and again in both European and African attacks on the Asian community. 'Further,' the petition said, 'the money earned by the natives of the country remains here, whereas the Asiatic takes away all his earnings to his native country . . . .'[22] Despite continuing efforts toward limiting the number of Indian immigrants during the early decades of this century, immigration control was one political battle the settlers were not to win.

Other suggested restrictions on Asian activities did obtain government endorsement. The most obvious economic proscriptions related to agriculture. Almost from the beginning of European settlement in East Africa, the Asians were discouraged from farming. A most effective way of excluding the Asians from this activity was to reserve the best agricultural land for the Europeans. In all three East African countries, land not held in trust for the African was alienated almost exclusively for European farmers. While a few of the more ingenious were able to circumvent the restrictions, the participation of Asians in agriculture was not to be as producers.

When attempts to accelerate European settlement in East Africa had only modest success, an emissary was sent to South Africa to recruit white farmers. The response was far more enthusiastic than had been hoped. The results of the subsequent influx of Boers was to have an important impact on the Indian in East Africa. The South Africans brought with them 'special views on race,'[23] and these views encouraged the deterioration of the Asians' status in the British territories.

Despite the recognition by many officials of the important role Indians were playing in the economy of East Africa, the basic suspicions that characterised the European attitude toward the Indian community on Zanzibar in the middle and late 1800s surfaced on the mainland shortly thereafter. In the span of less than a decade, three events occurred which exacerbated the negative attitudes toward the Asian community in British East Africa. First was the importation of the coolie labourers to build the railroad; second, the promotion of white settlement as a key to economic development; and third, the immigration of South African Boers.

During that same period, a racial layering for East Africa was being implemented that would remain in almost unaltered form for decades. The roles of African, Asian and European were being predetermined. The European was to be at the top, and the African at the bottom, with the Asians filling the middle-class void existing between the other two. It ultimately would take a second world war and the independence movement that followed to modify these roles.

While this basic picture held true in Uganda as well as in Kenya, one potential difference was arising even in those early days of British rule. Uganda, it was suggested, should remain as an African country. In practical terms, what did this mean? It meant that European settlement should be kept to a minimum. It meant also that land acquisition by all non-Africans must be discouraged and carefully controlled. It, in effect, meant that Asians initially would be limited in the nongovernmental sphere to such occupations as 'trader, craftsman, and clerk.'[24] But it also meant that the Indian trader would be dealing with African small farmers who were being encouraged to grow cash crops. The traders, through the introduction of a money economy, and through providing goods for purchase, would be a major agent of the African development.

In Uganda, as in the other East African countries, the Asians have dominated many economic activities. The economic role they played in Uganda was similar to that in Kenya and Tanganyika, yet modified somewhat by the peculiar status of Uganda in the eyes of the colonial regime. As noted above, the British Government decided early that Uganda was to be a country in which the interests of the indigenous inhabitants would be paramount. The route to an African Uganda, however, was not as straightforward and direct as government fiat.

The search started for a viable method of making Uganda self-supporting. Clearly, the answer would lie, as it did in other African colonial possessions, in the discovery of appropriate cash crops for the export trade. Plantation owners and African small farmers were encouraged to try a variety of crops. From this experimenting, cotton emerged as the most suitable crop for that time and that place; and the Africans proved it could be grown on their modest land holdings. The die was cast. The major economic development of Uganda indeed was to come through African peasant agriculture, not alien farmers. It is by no means certain that Asians would have taken up agriculture even if encouraged to do so. The success of the African small farmer in producing cotton, the major cash crop, virtually assured that the Asians would not be given much of an opportunity.

Sugar growing provided the most notable accomplishments of plantation agriculture in Uganda and the most notable exception to the general absence of Asians from crop agriculture. It provided also the base for two of the greatest fortunes of Uganda and East Africa. In 1924, Nanki Kalidas Mehta began a sugar plantation on 5,000 derelict acres in eastern Buganda.[25] The next year he built a refinery at Lugazi near Jinja. Despite a number of difficulties endemic to Uganda at that time, notably poor transportation and high labour costs, the venture was a success. A stable domestic market, the suitability of sugar as a plantation crop, and government assistance in customs, tariffs and transportation costs were combined with business acumen and the willingness of the Indian managers to accept lower wages. The Mehta economic empire had begun. In 1929, a second sugar factory was opened. Muljibhai Madhvani, following the Mehta lead, began an operation on 4,000 acres in Busoga. The death in 1971 of Jayant Madhvani, Muljibhai's eldest son, brought to public attention the breadth achieved by the Madhvani group of industries – sugar, textiles, steel, breweries, glassware – and the importance of these industries in Uganda.[26]

The cotton industry also provides a good example of the persistence and ingenuity of the Asian businessman in Uganda. Constrained against the growing of cotton, the Asians turned to the ginning and trading of Uganda's major export. Originally, the ginning was controlled by Europeans, and in order to protect these white entrepreneurs, and to promote an orderly expansion of the industry, the Government placed tight restrictions on the primary marketing of the cotton crop. The ginners, needing an assured supply of cotton, argued for protection against '"volatile" middlemen without a real stake in the country, who would cream off easy profits in good years, cheating gullible peasants, and would abandon Uganda in bad years.'[27]

Unfortunately, from the ginner's viewpoint, most government controls (e.g. licensing and price-fixing), favoured the traders who were, of course, almost all Asian. By the 1920s, the cotton industry, like the colonial society as a whole, had achieved a clear three-level, racial layering. The Africans were the producers; the Asians, the middlemen; and the Europeans, the ginners.

The most profound impact of the Asians upon Uganda, as upon all of Eastern Africa, came through their accomplishments in the commercial sphere. Indian merchants have dominated trade in Uganda since before the turn of the century. The most famous, Allidina Visram, working his way inland along the ancient Arab trading routes, reached Uganda in the 1890s. During the 1890s, Allidina had reached Kampala and other traders had spread their activities '. . . to Toro and the vicinity of the Congo Free State, to places in Bunyoro, and on the posts at which European or native soldiers were established in the Nile Province, besides opening bazaars at all the stations in the Eastern half of the Protectorate.'[28] Like elsewhere in East Africa, the traders found the field wide open. Almost all of the indigenous inhabitants except for some in Buganda were without commercial acumen.

As the century closed, the trade of interior East Africa still resembled that of centuries before.[29] Ivory remained the major export, although supplies were dwindling, and agricultural products still were of little consequence. Soon thereafter, following Allidina's lead, the traders in Uganda made an important move. They began to turn their attention from ivory to cotton.

The major encouragement to further Indian commercial activity came from the building of the railroad and the subsequent opening of the interior. Newly arrived traders from Gujerat joined with those from the older firms to expand Indian enterprise in Uganda. Indian shops (*dukas*) began appearing all across the British-controlled areas of Uganda. New *dukas* were introduced to compete with old *dukas* and the bigger firms moved into areas opened by small traders. Even early in the century, a glut of small traders (*dukawallas*) seemed to be a legitimate concern in some areas. And by no means were all of the merchants the inventive energetic types generally associated with Indian commerce in East Africa. A contemporary observer of the early traders noted: 'It is very hard to see how they expect to thrive, as almost every store is the exact counterpart of its neighbours. However, whether they trade or not seems to be a matter of complete indifference to the store-keeper, judging by the placid way in which he sits among his goods, and the nonchalant air he adopts when asked his prices.'[30]

Although the rural *dukawallas* were the most famous of the Asian entrepreneurs in East Africa, their numerical superiority steadily diminished in the face of African competition. African interest in shop-keeping picked up particularly during and after World War II. In a 1952 survey of retail trade in Uganda, it was discovered that most of the traders were not Asians but Africans.[31] For the big urban operations, the African competition presented little if any threat, but the *dukawallas* in some rural environments were more noticeably affected. In the late 1950s, the long-standing latent hostility toward the non-African traders burst into the open, manifesting itself in attacks on Asian shops and shopkeepers.

The Asian wholesaler, on the other hand, remained immune from African competitors. At the turn of the century, it was estimated that Asians controlled 80 to 90 per cent of the trade in East Africa. Sixty years later at the time of independence, the figures had altered only slightly. Perhaps most significant of all, ten years after the attainment of political freedom, the economy of Uganda remained solidly in the hands of Asians. Apart from the small African traders, the Asians still were estimated to control 80 per cent of the commercial sector. Even after independence, the basic long-standing alien domination of commerce was proving virtually impossible to crack.

Economic motivation consistently has been the driving force behind the Asian communities. It was the cause of the migrations to East Africa, and it explains in large measure the acceptance by the Asians of a middle-level role in the social and political life of Uganda. Asians displayed a good deal of diversity in economic activities and in most, achieved a high degree of accomplishment. As Elspeth Huxley, daughter of a white settler family and noted authority on East Africa, was to write when explaining their later expulsion: 'The trouble with Uganda's Asians is success.'[32] This economic success combined with the nature of their business contacts with the African, and their social exclusivity, created the hostility with which they were regarded by the Ugandan African. The Asians were able to get along with the Government, but not with the people.

Evolution of the Asian Communities in Uganda

By the early 1920s, over 5,000 Asians were in Uganda. The more recent immigrants began to assume the major Asian role, replacing the older generation Indian merchants in importance. Hindus, mainly from Gujerat, were becoming the largest group. The immigration was to continue into the 1950s, but since it was to come from the same areas that produced the influx in the century's first two decades, it changed the size but not the basic character of the Asian community.

The basic patterns which were to remain until World War II were well established. The three-levelled society based on racial castes was clearly delineated throughout East Africa. Uganda, like the other East African countries, had become a plural society. In race, language and function, the Asians were a community clearly distinguishable from the Europeans and Africans and were to remain so until their departure decades later.[33]

On most accounts, however, to label the variety of Asians in Uganda as a single community was misleading. Only in the early part of the century did the Asians, small in number, similar in occupation, and struggling to establish themselves, identify with other Asians irrespective of religion or caste. As the population grew through natural increase and immigration, the Ugandan Asian community began to break up into the component parts which were to characterise it from that point on. While all Asians might align themselves together for purposes of pursuing a particular political course of action, this became increasingly rare as the various Asian religious or sectarian groups grew large enough to be effective.

The desire for endogamous groups was founded on deeply-rooted beliefs brought from India. It was not considered arrogant or unfriendly to stick within one's own group. In no way did the Asians equate their desire for separatism with a lack of loyalty to the political system.[34] Within the confines of the colonial system the exclusivity not only was tolerated, but it also generally represented an advantage to the Government, reducing as it did the political effectiveness of the broader Asian community.

What factors promoted the growth of the multiplicity of Asian communities in Uganda and East Africa? H.S. Morris, in his book, *The Indians in Uganda,* suggests four.[35] First was the ease of communication between East Africa and India. Thus it was possible with even a small Asian population in East Africa to refrain from such intercaste contact and to retain the traditions of the group. Second was continuing growth of the Asian population. Third was the the presence of the Ismaili community as a 'pace-making' group. The followers of the Aga Khan, generally the most westernised, independent, and, some would argue, progressive Asian group, established their own identity very early in East Africa and by their success encouraged others to do the same. Fourth, men of ambition found that the quickest route to power was through these communities and, in turn, supported their separate development.

Two other factors of a negative quality tended to discourage the formation of a single Ugandan Asian community. No institutions had been brought from India to East Africa that would act to unite the entire Asian or, for that matter, Hindu or Muslim, communities.

Additionally, in Uganda the racial difficulties were less inflammatory than in other areas of East Africa. The relative good will reduced the incentive and need for a unified Asian front in that country.

Within the racial caste, a product of the colonial society in which they lived, the Asians formed a complex pattern of religious and sectarian communities.[36] The isolation that resulted from the colonial tripartite division suited the Asians in many ways. Isolation certainly was reinforced by the '. . . general compartmentalisation of the Indian community into religious, communal, sectional, and caste groups. . . .'[37]

Why did the Asians accept the concept and implementation of a plural society as readily as they did? Why did they do so little to try to alter the economic, political, and social segregation that resulted?

One reason was their lack of political consciousness and clout. Coming as they did from an area of white domination, they were more ready to accept it as a fact of life. Many Indians may have even believed in the theory of European supremacy. Beyond that, in Uganda they had neither the colonial regime nor the strength of numbers to support their political aims. Political inactivity may only have resulted from deeper motivations the Asians had for accepting the colonial *fait accompli*.

Socially, the racial castes suited the communal-minded Asians. Laws supporting racial segregation acted in concert with traditional beliefs to aid the Asians' attempt at cultural separatism. Additionally, the constraints placed on Asian economic enterprise, political and social roles made entry into the colonial society easier for the new immigrants. Unlike the situation in many migrations, the new arrivals had to deal with neither racial conflict nor competition.[38]

After the defeat of early and active attempts to achieve parity with the European community, the East African Asians pragmatically accepted their position in the middle stratum. The Asian sphere was defined far more broadly in East Africa than it was in South Africa where the Asians also formed an important minority group. The economic opportunities afforded by this more liberal stance were rich indeed, and the Asians were to make the most of them. And if the tri-level policy prevented the Asians from climbing into the white sphere in East Africa, it also protected the Asian stratum from the designs of the Africans.

It was predictable that cultural influences from the indigenous Africans would be minimal. The Asians felt superior to the Africans and cut themselves off from the latter's culture. In Uganda, even the relatively ubiquitous Swahili language, one of the major indigenous culture contributions, was learned less enthusiastically than elsewhere in East Africa.[39]

More surprising is the lack of European cultural influence among the Asians. While the European technological impact has been profound in East Africa, other cultural influence has been much less so, less even than that on the Indian subcontinent itself. This latter aspect makes it unlikely that a feeling of cultural superiority among the East African Asians has contributed to the dearth of European impact. More likely, it was the nature of the British population in Uganda, Tanzania, and Kenya that made the culture impact minimal. Civil servants, soldiers, businessmen and farmers, it has been suggested, have neither the motivation nor the means to act as ambassadors of European culture. Add to this the general lack of contact between the races plus the separative nature of the Asian communities, and the arguments against assimilation of western culture are weighty ones.

Education was one area in which western influence increased steadily. As the various Asian communities grew, it was natural that they would establish their own schools. The substantial weight of the Asian resources devoted to education thus was spread thinly over many different institutions. In Uganda, this contributed to the initially poor quality of many Asian schools. For example, in 1935, only 8 per cent of the Indian teachers were graduates of Indian universities.[40]

Later, the increases in government supervision of Indian education resulted in the establishment of modern, English-system schools by the end of World War II. Standards and facilities improved even further during the post-war period, especially in secondary education. Government grants for education matched the substantial contributions of the Asian communities themselves.[41]

The concern for educational quality and the size of investments made to achieve it, reflects the great interest and faith the Asian community had in education. Recognising the economic gains that accrue to those with sufficient schooling, many Asian families set aside a considerable portion of their savings to send a son or sons to Britain for technical training or a university degree.

Western-style education was not an unmixed blessing for the Asian families. The traditional parochial schools included Asian religious values in the curriculum, while the nonparochial public or private schools did not. The European-type schools also tended to create a communications breakdown between the students and the older generations at home.[42] The most recent generation of East African Asians has been the first to undergo, almost exclusively, western-style schooling. Older generations, if formally educated, went through Asian parochial schools. Those educated in the European-type schools found their ties becoming stronger with their schoolmates than with their 'nonwesternised' kin.

The degree of acculturation to western influence varied not only from activity to activity but also from generation to generation, and from community to community. The newer the generation, the more likely that its members had been exposed to European-style education, either in East Africa or in Britain with the resulting consequences. The variation in acculturation from community to community was substantial. The Khoja Ismailis, by almost any criterion, lead in the degree of acceptance of western models of behaviour.[43] The Punjabis and Sikhs rank high on such a scale while the other Muslims, the Jains and the Shahs would show the lowest degree of acculturation. The Gujerati Hindus, comprising a large percentage of the Asian population, would be in the middle.

It is remarkable that despite the conservatism of Muslim communities, generally the Ismailis are the most westernised. This, without doubt, remains attributable to the leadership of the Aga Khan. His Highness consistently encouraged the Ismaili community to adopt western ways — such encouragement sometimes taking the form of religious decrees.

Another westernised group are the Goans. These people, originating in the former Portuguese enclave on India's west coast, resisted being classified as Asians or Indians. In this, they were somewhat successful, as the Goans at times were listed officially as distinct from the Asians in East Africa. Often of mixed descent (Portuguese and Indian), the Goans typically are Roman Catholic and English speaking.

Political activity of Asians in East Africa has been marked by three characteristics: (1) lack of unity; (2) lack of initiative; and (3) lack of leadership. Reasons for the lack of unity in the Asian community have been outlined above. An explanation for the basic Asian policy of 'response' politics is less direct. The lack of initiative probably resulted from apolitic naiveté among the immigrants; an acceptance of British rule, with the community having emigrated from a British-dominated area; and the economic successes being achieved by the Asians. A big political disappointment was the failure of leaders to arise who could span the religious and secular boundaries of the communities. Most Asians of political ambition found, as mentioned earlier, that the best route to influence the colonial government was through leadership in their own group and not through the broader Asian community.

To combat the growing anti-Indian feeling and the increasingly unsympathetic attitude of the local government, the Eastern African Indian National Congress was formed, meeting for the first time in Mombasa in 1914. Its goal was to promote the 'complete and full' equality of the Indians with other immigrant communities. The Asians already had lost the right to obtain land from the Government in most parts of Kenya and Uganda. In 1915 the Crown Lands Ordinance gave the Government veto power over land transfer between members of different races. Asian purchase of agricultural land had been, for all intents and purposes, eliminated.

The decade immediately following the First World War was a politically stormy period for Asians in East Africa. The battle was joined with the Government in Kenya over what the European community called 'irreducible minimums':

(1) strictly controlled immigration of Indians leading ultimately to prohibition;
(2) two nominated (not elected) Indians on legislative council in Kenya;
(3) segregation in residential areas (and, when possible, commercial);
(4) no alienation of lands to Asians in Highlands;
(5) no franchise to Indians.

The outcome of this struggle was the White Paper of 1923. The Asians had achieved some measure of success. Five Asians were to be elected to the legislative council but under a communal system; the proposed policy of segregation in towns was abandoned; and immigration was not to be restricted on racial grounds. Still the Asians had not obtained the desired parity with the white community. Many saw the White Paper as a political defeat for the Asian community — a defeat that would have ramifications for not only the Kenya Asians, but for all those in East Africa.[44]

While it would be misleading to suggest that the Asian communities withdrew from the political arena in Uganda, their impact was sporadic. They would be plagued persistently by the lack of unified voice. The Asians did form the Central Council of Indian Associations. While generally standing in opposition to racial discrimination, the Council could not agree to a common position on such basic issues as land policy for cemeteries and places of worship.[45] The Council failed to gain support from the sects and was thus, in most cases, ineffectual.

By the 1930s, the Ugandan Asians had accepted the idea of communal representation and had representatives serving on the legislative council. The basic political strategy among the Asian communities had become, and would remain, one of compromise. This proved to be a wise policy during the days of the British rule because it solidified the economically dominant status of the Asians.

After World War II the political separation of India and Pakistan had repercussions in Uganda. The Muslims demanded separate seats in the legislative council and formed a separate political organisation. During this same period, the Asian communities began to recognise the need to establish new relationships with the rising African political leaders. Many Asians now saw independence for Uganda as inevitable and the implications of the demise of colonial rule, while not clear, seemed ominous.

Nationalism was not a new idea or experience for the Asians. They had supported the orderly move toward self-government in India. In Uganda, leaders of the Asian communities raised their voices in support of independence, but fears for the future began to modulate their enthusiasm. This Asian ambivalence about the demise of colonial — and the rise of African — rule was understandable, but it predictably produced anger among the Black Ugandans.

As independence approached, the Asians grew increasingly uneasy. While some Asian leaders continued to support nationalist causes, that support was not always received with enthusiasm by the Africans. The Asians, knowing that the revolution was at hand, worried about the preservation of the 'economic status quo.' Clearly, the favoured social and political position they enjoyed in the colonial era was to be no more. This, most Asians could consider acceptable. Would independence mean, however, that their traditional economic role would also be changed? That was a price Ugandan Asians would not wish to pay.

The Years of Independence

Despite their many reservations, the Asians made the transition from British to African rule in good style. They displayed toward independence the same adaptability and resignation that had been so characteristic throughout their history in East Africa. Independence did change substantially the character, if not the scope, of Asian political activity. The tri-level racial policy of colonial days was dead. The theory of racial superiority, and the basic tenet of divide and rule — both valuable to colonial control — were antithetical to the new Government's search to unite the diverse elements in their countries. The Asian communities no longer could exist as political entities.

Of more practical and immediate concern to the East African Asians was the question of citizenship. It was to become a complicated, emotional and unnerving matter for the next decade. And answers would be generated not only in Kampala, but in London as well. As Uganda struggled with the matter of citizenship for minority races, the British developed a strategy for accepting minority immigrants.

Contemporaneously with the implementation of the 1968 British Immigration Act, President Obote set about rectifying the Asian domination of commerce in Uganda. This domination was unacceptable to the Ugandan Government for two reasons in particular: (1) The Asians were continuing to send money out of the country primarily to the United Kingdom,[46] and (2) the Africans could not expect to gain economic control of their own country as long as the Asian commercial dominance continued.

The President's strategy was twofold. He placed regulations on the residential status of noncitizens in Uganda and restricted the commercial activities of the Asians under a Traders' Licensing Act. Shortly thereafter, Dr Obote also unveiled plans for the nationalisation of some major business enterprises. After a surprise announcement of the Government's intentions, the President revealed a detailed strategy for the takeover.

In all of these actions, the President suggested reasonable timetables for implementation. The rate of prospective Asian deportation under the regulations appeared to match Britain's acceptance rate under the 1968 Immigration Act. The actual implementation of Obote's plans unfortunately was chaotic and confused; many Asians eventually ignored the provisions of the legislation.

The Asians obviously were not pleased with the President's ideas about an African takeover. They welcomed the military coup of January 1971 in which the deposed Obote was replaced by General Amin. Britain received the news with 'ill-concealed relief,'[47] hoping to get a better deal on Asian immigrants from Amin than they had from Obote.

Less than a year later, the Asians began to regret the change in Ugandan leadership. In October, Amin ordered a census of all Asians regardless of their citizenship status. Then on December 7–8, he called a conference of representatives of the entire Asian community. In a scathing denunciation of the Asians, Amin took them to task for their lack of faith in his government, their exploitation of the African, and their social exclusivity.

The Asian community delivered a powerful reply, and the situation quieted noticeably. Amin did not answer the Asian leaders, and no action was taken by the Government. The Asians, justifiably, decided to let well enough alone.

After almost eight months of quiescence, the President struck. On July 30, speaking at the opening of two buildings at Uganda College of Commerce in Kampala, Amin addressed an old and familiar theme. He said that 'our industry and commerce are being manned by foreigners.'[48] Despite the reopening of the verbal warfare, there were no indications that he was yet ready to take any dramatic step to change that situation.

Then on August 1, a story appeared on page 3 of the *Argus*.

A meeting of all traders in Bukedi District is to be held today at the Rock View School, Tororo.

According to the District Commissioner, Mr B. Kato, the meeting will be in response to a directive given by a government spokesman that traders in all districts in Uganda should meet to draft a memorandum to President Amin.

Mr Kato says that all traders in Bukedi had been asked to leave their businesses and attend 'this very important meeting in the history of trades in the district.' He emphasised that the meeting should be attended by Ugandan citizens only.[49]

The story further mentioned that landlords were telling tenants of a 'major renovation' which was due to take place soon.[50] There may have been no official connection between the language used in the announcement and the statements which were to emanate from the President later. One can speculate, however, that grassroots support was being generated in order to provide for a most enthusiastic response to the forthcoming edict.

Two days later, the only news in the *Argus* about Asians was a picture of the official opening of a newly remodelled Lions Club in Masaka.[51] Asians, it would appear, were going about business as usual. They, like the rest of the Ugandan population, seemed unaware of the momentous times ahead.

On the fateful day, the secret was still a well-kept one. The *East African Standard*'s lead article on August 4 concerned the crisis in Britain resulting from the prolonged longshoremen's strike, while the *Argus* headlined its front page with a story of the disillusionment of the two Uganda boxers who had failed to make the Olympic team.[52] Both newspapers did carry stories of the increasing pressure being brought on Britain to issue special entry vouchers for East African Asian passport holders attempting to enter Britain from India. And that was the issue that some authorities argue triggered Amin's decree. Ironically, the article suggested that whatever modifications the British Foreign Office might be willing to make in order to quiet that increasingly sensitive issue, it would certainly not reduce the 3,000 vouchers issued annually to Kenya, Uganda and Tanzania. The agreement on that quota had 'at last overcome years of [immigration] difficulty in East Africa.'[53] Whitehall clearly did not want to provoke the Uganda Government on the issue of Asian migration from Uganda to Britain.

On that same day, August 4, the President made public his plan to rid Uganda of the Asians. The wheels of deportation began to turn, and what the Asians had built with care and immense effort, abruptly was toppling. The Asians faced the inevitability of the end of their East African world.

Final Days in Kampala

As the implication of Amin's actions became apparent, the level of excitement and concern among the Asians increased. Their first task was to clarify legal status and, if necessary, begin the processing for departure.

Those lining up at the immigration office were attempting to have their Ugandan citizenship verified. The majority were failing. Various technicalities were being employed to render these Ugandan passport holders stateless.

Even more unsuccessful were attempts by smaller numbers of British Asians to obtain exemptions from the decree. Despite his earlier statements that people in certain professions could remain, Amin, two weeks later, had changed his mind because they 'could not serve in good spirit after the departure of the other Asians.' Asians who had considered Uganda their lifetime home were being turned out on the streets of the world.

At the High Commission, the wait was for British passports and entry vouchers. To augment the beleaguered staff in Kampala, the Foreign Office sent a team of immigration personnel along with experts in employment and property valuation.

On August 21 the President cancelled his order to expel all Asians from Uganda, regardless of their citizenship. Only the noncitizens were to go. By so doing, he relieved some of the pressure on officials who would be organising the departure. More importantly from Amin's standpoint, the distinction he finally drew between citizen and non-citizen Asians was aimed at erasing the racist label which some African leaders and the world press had affixed to the expulsion decree. Unfortunately, of the 23,000 or so Asians who had declared for Uganda citizenship, only about half would be able to meet the deadline for checking their claims. For a time at least, the others would be in a state of limbo.

On the same day, the British High Commission announced it would begin issuing entry certificates for 3,000 heads-of-household. The bittersweet announcement forced upon the Asian community the realisation that Britain had accepted the Amin decree. There now appeared no escaping its consequences.

For the first 3,000 certificate holders and their dependents, the shock may not have been so profound. They had already applied for permission to enter the United Kingdom before the decision of August 4. Yet under normal circumstances, applicants typically had to wait two to three years to enter Britain. It is likely that even of those who already had applied, few were near enough to closing their affairs in Uganda to allow them to leave without absorbing some degree of financial loss.

All departing Asians had to undergo clearance by both British and Ugandan officials. The process was not functioning smoothly, and blame was laid on all sides. The Asians levelled accusations at both the British High Commission and the Ugandan Government of operating too slowly. The High Commission replied that many passport holders were not appearing for clearance on their scheduled days. Ugandan officials said that by mid-September, 1,500 exit vouchers were being issued daily.[54] Asians, waiting in line for days at the Bank of Uganda for airline tickets, claimed the figure was less than 100 per day.

Some of the complexities of departure related to registration forms for Asian businesses. The owners were required to list assets — property, buildings, and businesses — along with current stocks of merchandise and goods already ordered. No compensation could be gained if the forms were not completed.

By mid-September, processing still was not at a pace which would instil confidence in on-time departures for the Asians. Notices appeared in newspapers, suggesting in forceful terms that Asians should have documentation taken care of as quickly as possible. These announcements raised a storm of protest from the Asians, who once again claimed High Commission 'foot-dragging.' Ironically, they appealed to the Ugandan Government to exert pressure on the British.

At the same time, British officials were becoming concerned with the small numbers of Asians that were coming to the airports. By September 20, about 8,000 possessed clearance to embark for England, but very few had done so.

The reluctance related in no small way to the treatment received by earlier departees during the bus trip from Kampala to the airport at Entebbe. Many of the Asians were stopped at numerous control points, searched at gunpoint, and had valuables, including jewelry, confiscated. Another, and perhaps more important, motive for delaying departure was the last desperate hope that some business deals could be concluded in order to salvage some measure of financial resource. Also, the unsettled situation of the stateless Asians kept some of their concerned relatives behind to keep tabs on their welfare.

After a period of confusion and negotiation, Amin agreed that East African Airways — his initial choice to handle the entire airlift — would share the job with two British airlines. The migrant fare was set at 2,000 Ugandan shillings, which was substantially higher than earlier estimates.

The refugees had no choice. They were forced to pay their own way, just as they themselves, or their forebears, did when immigrating to East Africa. As in that earlier immigration, many would turn to the Asian community for help in raising the necessary money. The number of Asians without sufficient funds steadily increased. Work permits were withdrawn at a rate faster than immigration from Uganda to Britain could be achieved. As the jobless waited for their turn, their resources steadily dwindled.

On September 17, the first 'immigrant special' left Uganda with 193 on board. Its departure signalled the beginning of the major airlift which was obligated to remove all British Asians from Uganda by November 7. As planes departed with less than capacity loads, fears of a logistical crisis increased. General Amin offered encouragement for speedy departures by first suggesting that any Asians not meeting the deadline would be put in camps, and later ordering that all aliens cleared for departure by Uganda authorities must leave the country within forty-eight hours of that clearance. Fears and frustrations among the Asians intensified. By early October, the military began checking Asian buildings to see that all noncitizens were departing on schedule. The prodding by the Government had its effect and the airlift increased in tempo. On 25th October 1972, the British High Commission placed its final announcement to the Asians in the Uganda papers:

> If you hold a United Kingdom passport and are a head of a family, an independent person, or the wife of a Ugandan, Indian or stateless husband and have not come forward for an entry certificate, you must do so now.[54]

Not all of the Asians leaving Uganda were going to Britain. A number of nations agreed to take some of the stateless. Canada alone processed almost 8,000. India agreed to accept up to 15,000 British Asians, but only under a similar triangle deal as had been worked out in 1968 for the Kenyan Asians. India would provide a temporary home, if Britain would honour its obligations to accept the Asians at a later date.

Most of the British Asians, of course, had gone to the United Kingdom, and the movement of the immigrants was a major accomplishment.

Despite the confusion, the lack of cooperation, and the vagaries of the Uganda Government, the November 8 deadline was met. On that signal day, the attitudes of Britain and Uganda toward the expulsion were worlds apart. The *Times* headlined its editorial 'The Tragedy of Uganda,' while the *Argus*' front page rejoiced with the news that at last Uganda was free. The Asians were leaving a hostile Uganda. How would they be received when they arrived in Britain? Reports from the United Kingdom gave them cause for both hope and apprehension. Were the Asians about to face, as one bitter Ugandan had wished them, 'a long and very cold winter,'[55] or would the British 'make a success story of this involuntary transplantation of human skills, energies and cultural diversity?'[56]

Notes

1. For further elaboration of the Asians' background in India, see for example: J.S. Mangat, *A History of the Asians in East Africa* (London, 1969); D. Ghai and Y. Ghai (eds), *Portrait of a Minority* (Nairobi, 1970); G. Delf, *Asians in East Africa* (London, 1962).

2. S.S. Mangat, *op. cit.*, p. 1.
3. K. Ingham, *A History of East Africa* (New York, 1965), p. 6.
4. The importance of that post can be judged from the fact that nine-tenths of the sultan's revenues came from customs duties.
5. R. Coupland, *The Exploitation of East Africa* (London, 1968) p. 202.
6. G. Delf, *op. cit.*, p. 62.
7. R. Robinson and J. Gallagher, *Africa and the Victorians* (London, 1961), p. 464.
8. C.F. Andrews, *The Indian Question in East Africa* (Nairobi, 1921), p. 2.
9. That appellation was employed on many occasions during the century following Burton's statement, most recently in President Idi Amin's attacks on the Ugandan Asian community.
10. Mangat, *op. cit.*, p. 22.
11. *Ibid.*, pp. 24-5.
12. As quoted by A.B. Patel in the Presidential Address to the Eastern Africa Indian National Congress, 15th session, Nairobi, December 31, 1938.
13. C. Miller, *The Lunatic Express* (New York, 1971), p. 173.
14. The *Times*, October 6, 1899.
15. Decades later the myth served another purpose. It was used as ammunition in the arguments over whether Britain was or was not ultimately responsible for the Asians, who, under newly independent governments, were finding cause to leave East Africa.
16. In South Africa, a social distinction is drawn between 'passenger' Indians, i.e. those who paid their own way, and persons of indentured stock. H. Kuper, *Indian People in Natal* (Durban, 1960), pp. 7-9.
17. Sir H. Johnston as quoted in R. Oliver, *Sir Harry Johnston and the Scramble for Africa* (London, 1957), p. 293.
18. Mangat, *op. cit.*, p. 39.
19. Ingham, *op. cit.*, p. 216.
20. While the White Highlands of Kenya were to be a major political issue a half-century later in the African's march to independence, the European efforts to keep these areas exclusively for their use had been designed essentially to prevent Asian settlement. E. Soja, *The Geography of Modernization in Kenya* (Syracuse, 1968), pp. 22-23.
21. Sir Charles Eliot, *East African Protectorate* (London, 1905), p. 3.
22. As quoted in Mangat, *op. cit.*, p. 98.
23. H.S. Morris, *The Indians in Uganda* (Chicago, 1968), p. 10.
24. *Ibid.*, p. 12.
25. Ehrlich, 'The Uganda Economy' in V. Harlow, *et al.* (eds), *The History of East Africa* (London, 1965), vol. 2, p. 433.
26. Jayant's death also brought these comments from President Amin: 'Jayant will be missed by all who knew him, more especially so for what he lived and worked for and for the stirring example he has given to the society of various races such as our own. Jayant has been a great son of Uganda whose activities and ways of life will always be remembered.' President Idi Amin, 'mourning message on the death of Jayant Madhvani' as quoted in *East African Standard*, 6 August 1971.
27. Ehrlich, *op. cit.*, p. 438.
28. H.H. Johnston, *The Uganda Protectorate* (London, 1902), p. 294.
29. With the exception, of course, of slaves.
30. C.W. Hattersley, *The Buganda at Home*, p. 85 as quoted in Ehrlich, *op. cit.*, p. 408.
31. Dept. of Commerce Annual Report, 1952, p. 5, as quoted in Morris, *op. cit.*, p. 145.

32. E. Huxley, 'England Faces the Great Migration,' *National Review*, October 13, 1972, p. 1124.
33. Morris, *op. cit.*, p. 161.
34. D. Ghai and Y. Ghai, 'Historical Introduction' in Ghai and Ghai (eds), *op. cit.*, p. 11.
35. Morris, *op. cit.*, pp. 40-41.
36. For a recent evaluation of the Asian communities in East Africa, see A. A. Bharati, *The Asians in East Africa* (Chicago, 1972).
37. Mangat, *op. cit.*, p. 142.
38. Y. Ghai, 'The Future Prospects' in Ghai and Ghai, *op. cit.*, pp. 180-181.
39. This may reflect the more limited use of Swahili as a *lingua franca* in Uganda than in Tanzania or Kenya.
40. Delf, *op. cit.*, p. 27.
41. Mangat, *op. cit.*, pp. 173-174.
42. A. Gharati, 'A Social Survey' in Ghai and Ghai, *op. cit.*, p. 64.
43. For reasons mentioned below, ranking of the Goans presents a particular problem. The Goans think of themselves as 'western' and, in many ways, would have to be considered so.
44. On the other hand, the Asians had helped prevent Kenya and perhaps all of East Africa from becoming an area in which White interests would be paramount. For this reason, some people consider this struggle the Asians' major political accomplishment in East Africa.
45. Morris, *op. cit.*, p. 33.
46. President Amin was later to suggest that more money was going from Uganda to the United Kingdom via this method than Uganda was receiving in financial assistance from Britain.
47. The *Times*, August 7, 1972.
48. *Uganda Argus*, July 31, 1972.
49. *Uganda Argus*, August 1, 1972.
50. *Ibid.*
51. *Ibid.*, August 3, 1972.
52. *East African Standard*, August 4, 1973 and *Uganda Argus*, August 4, 1973.
53. The *Times*, September 15, 1972.
54. *Ibid.*
55. *Uganda Argus*, October 25, 1972.
56. Reverend Peter Ben Ochan, letter to *Uganda Argus*, August 18. 1972.
57. The *Times*, November 8, 1972.

3. BRITISH LEGACY AND RESPONSE

By the end of August, the mood of the British public at its best could be described as sullen, and at its worst, hostile. The full impact of another wave of immigrants began to reverberate among 'native' British. The London *Sunday Telegraph* spoke to the highly critical popular reaction in Great Britain:

> A further large swift influx of coloured immigrants to Britain is wholly undesirable on social grounds. . . . The Ugandan emergency must affect our ability to take any further immigration for the foreseeable future. If there are complaints, let them be addressed to President Amin and the blame put squarely at the door of black racialism.[1]

The leading spokesman in Great Britain for white supremacy, Mr Enoch Powell, a Conservative MP, brutally attacked his own Government's policy:

> Evidently few of those who are shocked, and rightly shocked at the prospect of 50,000 Asians from Uganda being added to our population have any idea that 40,000 a year are still being admitted year in and year out and that in every single succeeding year, about a hundred thousand are added, through immigration and natural increase, to the coloured population of this country.[2]

Mr Powell was quick to add that Britain should provide assistance to the oppressed and take her due share, but when a group of people are being exiled, all countries should take their share in accordance with size, opportunities and affinity.[3]

Four hundred demonstrators turned out in London to protest the 'invasion of Britain' by Ugandan Asians. Carrying signs saying 'STOP Immigration, Enoch is Right' and 'Britain for the British,' meat porters, dockers, and a right-wing political organisation marched on the Home Office. According to *Times* reports, the marchers 'sang "Rule Britannia" with a specially amended line, "Britain, never, never, never, will be spades" and outside both Rhodesia House and South Africa House the marchers cheered.'[4]

The Ugandan Asian crisis found the British Isles in a rather extended period of net out-migration. In a crowded nation, this should be a positive sign — but to the British it was not. The reason is basic: the out-migration is composed mainly of whites; the immigration is almost entirely nonwhite. The British leaving for distant shores head for the older Dominions (the 'white' Dominions) of Canada, South Africa, New Zealand and Australia. Those immigrants arriving in Britain come from the new Dominions, especially those of the Indian subcontinent and the West Indies.

The emigration of whites represents a continuation of a massive movement of the British to overseas domains. That migration began in the seventeenth century, reached its zenith in the 1800s, and persists to this day. It was, in some measure, a conscious part of an imperial strategy which created what most British leaders considered the most important and dependable components of the Empire. Much of the emigration however, was accomplished with neither Government blessing nor support.[5]

The migration of nonwhite Commonwealth citizens to Britain is, of course, a much more recent development. Almost all have arrived since the partition of India and many since the independence of the African colonies. The extent of the coloured immigration was alarming Britain and contributed substantially to the uneasiness concerning the arrival of the Asians from Uganda. The coloured population in England and Wales was approaching 1 million in the late 1960s and has increased steadily since that time.[6] This increase was occurring in spite of actions Britain has taken to reduce the amount of that influx.

Unfortunately for the Ugandan Asians, and for the British, the crisis arose at a time which hardly could be called quiet or uneventful in the United Kingdom. In addition to the longstanding immigration difficulties, a combination of impending Common Market entry, persistent problems in Northern Ireland, shortages of housing, mounting inflation, a long and unpleasant dock strike, and continued unemployment had created an environment hardly conducive to the ready acceptance of many thousands of nonwhite refugees. 'Why,' the British were asking, 'are we responsible while the rest of the world remains aloof? Why must the burden be upon our shoulders?'

Placing the British bitterness and anxiety about the Uganda influx in perspective, *The Guardian* on August 19 reminded its readers: 'What we are seeing is the flotsam and jetsam of the imperial era which somehow never seems to get completely tidied up.'[7] Clearly, Britain's responsibility to the refugees was yet another painful reminder of an empire that was gone. And the mood in the United Kingdom during the uneasy days of 1972 could be traced in no small measure to conditions intimately associated with the demise of that empire.

The Imperial Legacy

Britain's empire was the greatest the modern world has seen.[8] Historians argue over the motives behind the assemblage of such an empire. Whether 'like Topsy' or by grand design, the British presence expanded continually after the defeat of Napoleon, and with it the establishment of British paramountcy in Europe and on the oceans of the world.[9] Britain seemed a rather reluctant imperial power during parts of the 1800s.[10] Yet inexorably during the century, her influence was spread through the emigration to new worlds of her sons and daughters, through foreign trade, through diplomacy, and indeed, where necessary, through imperial might. While the desire to add colonies was not a consistent goal of the British, the empire grew nevertheless. Then in the final quarter of the century, it exploded in size.

The last great area of the earth to which no claim had been laid by Europe was tropical Africa. For reasons that in many cases had little to do with the characteristics or desirability of the areas involved, Europe divided up the continent. In a remarkable display of diplomacy, the imperial nations negotiated boundaries and parcelled out Africa. The British took large chunks of west, south-central, and east Africa and set about the task of occupying them and making them as economically viable as possible. In East Africa, as noted above, the Asians from British India were major contributors to the process.

As the end of the Victorian era approached and the Asians began to migrate to East Africa in substantial numbers, Britain was the supreme imperial power in the world. In the near century since Waterloo, her empire grew to encompass a quarter of the population and the land area of the world. That empire had become, in fact, one on which the sun never set. With supremacy in Europe and dominion of the seas, the British Empire could approach the coming century with a substantial and seemingly justifiable confidence.[11]

Yet as the 1900s began, Britain was involved in the greatest colonial war it had yet fought. Over 500,000 redcoat soldiers were committed in South Africa against the Boers. Ultimately, the British prevailed as they had prevailed in all of their major imperial enterprises of the 1800s, but the war, however, was not a popular one and was a precursor of difficult decades ahead for the empire.

The Second World War was to take a particularly large toll. The resources expended by Britain were enormous, and the nation's economy suffered. Control over the empire on which Britain had come to depend was severely weakened. Serious defeats inflicted on European forces by non-Caucasians in Asia early in the war called into doubt the supposed superiority of the Western nations. Coloured colonial troops fighting for the British Empire began to question just whose freedom was being defended. Once again Britain emerged from the war on the winning side, but in the process she lost her leadership of the world and, as it turned out, was about to lose her empire.

After the war, some British politicians saw their nation's problems as short-term ones created by the war. Others recognised that they were of a more durable nature – that the imperial domain was passing. Independence movements, long submerged or suppressed in the colonies, surfaced in this post-war period. First to go was the 'kingpin' of the empire, British India. With the subdivision of the subcontinent in 1947, Britain relinquished control over what many considered her most important domain. As the empire began to disappear, the Commonwealth, designed by the British as its successor, began to grow. India and Pakistan, followed a year later by Ceylon, were the charter members of what later was to be dubbed the 'New Commonwealth.' The independence of Britain's African possessions created the most dramatic increase in the size of the 'New Commonwealth' membership. Thirteen nations from that continent alone were added in less than a decade. These new members included the three East African countries.

The growth of the Commonwealth and the shrinking of the empire had important implications for Britain. While the advantages of imperial power were declining, many of the old obligations persisted. These obligations included pumping British resources into the fragile economies of a number of ex-colonies. The economy of the 'mother country' got into deeper and deeper trouble in the decades after World War II, and financial assistance to the New Commonwealth became a serious drain on Britain.

Despite the continuing decline of Britain's political power and economic strength, the nation struggled to meet its obligations and to fulfil the responsibilities which the world community felt that Britain owed to the Commonwealth. It would be unrealistic to suggest that Britain's economic difficulties resulted from its Commonwealth commitments, but it is true that many of the problems could be traced to dependence on an empire that had disappeared. The dependence on the British Empire was by no means restricted to Britain alone. Many of its component states relied on British financial assistance for their growth, on British law for their stability, and on British strength for their defence. Being British was for many of these states and their citizens as good an assurance of safe conduct through the troubled world as could be offered. Later this confidence was to become as anachronistic as the empire itself.

No people in the empire, or in the Commonwealth, depended more on the maintenance of British prominence in the old empire structure than the East African Asians.[12] They arrived in East Africa at the height of British world power, and they assumed their designated place in a British colonial society. Their role in that society was protected by colonial rule, and they held what they believed was the ultimate guarantee against future difficulties – British citizenship. The Asians remained aloof from the newly independent governments, secure in the belief that the British could keep things from getting too bad; and if somehow their position in East Africa became intolerable, they could always and immediately go to Britain. But the British could not prevent the Asians' world from collapsing in Uganda; and like those from Kenya before them, the Ugandan Asians were to find their entry into the United Kingdom not nearly as simple as they expected.

Immigration Strategies

Immigration has been and still remains the most complicated and controversial matter in Britain's relationship with the other Commonwealth countries. When Britain first legally recognised the independence of Commonwealth countries in 1931, the total membership was five — Britain and the four white Dominions: Australia, New Zealand, Canada and South Africa. In this period, immigration to Britain from the other Commonwealth countries was not large. Additionally, it was almost entirely white. At the time of Indian independence, the British redefined the laws on citizenship in the British Nationality Act of 1948. In it, the citizens of any Commonwealth country (including the United Kingdom and colonies) had the status of either 'British subject' or 'Commonwealth citizen.' Britain hoped that the new act would secure equal rights and privileges for all people of the Commonwealth. The old (white) Dominions would have no part of that suggestion and retained long-standing discriminatory immigration policies; but Britain's doors were open.

The demise of the empire and the numerical increase in Commonwealth nations and citizens prompted the British to write a new Commonwealth Immigration Act in 1962. For the first time, Commonwealth passport holders would be subject to British immigration control. As independence was at hand for the East African countries, British ministers concerned over the fate of British white settlers there, moved to provide those colonials with an escape clause in the Act. The exemption was intended to provide that, in such nations as Uganda, the whites could choose to retain British citizenship and thus could renounce the opportunity for citizenship in the new nations.

Most ministers were aware that the clause providing such an alternative for European settlers could also be made available to East African Asians. It was suggested that careful drafting of the document could exclude nonwhites from the opportunity of choosing British citizenship, but Whitehall's legal experts vetoed an effort to that end. Proponents of the more general escape clause remained adamant, and led by the powerful and persuasive Duncan Sandys, they had their way. The clause was in, the white settlers were protected, and so too were the Asians.

The British Government had managed to provide an escape route to the white settlers but, 'by one of history's many ironies, British settlers in Kenya have not, as yet, been dispossessed or persecuted, whereas Uganda's Asians have.'[13] Was there any doubt in the minds of the ministers that they had provided a blank cheque to the Asians? Iain Macleod, speaking later to that point, made it clear — no doubt had existed. 'We did it. We meant to do it,' he said.[14]

The Asians in Uganda were then faced with the perplexity of deciding whether or not to accept Britain's offer. For the Ismaili community, the choice was clear. The Ismailis had been urged repeatedly by the Aga Khan to consider East Africa their home. When the time came, they opted overwhelmingly for East African citizenship.

The remaining Asians deliberated as hard and as long as possible. Loyalty to the new nation or to the old was weighed only lightly on the scale. It was rather a matter of business, 'as if nationality was a commodity in the market.'[15] Many eventually chose to 'go for Britain'. In Uganda, where the total Asian population had traditionally been the smallest in the East African nations, less than one-third elected Ugandan citizenship.

As the anticipated 'Africanisation' of political, governmental and economic endeavours accelerated in the mid-1960s, the tempo of emigration of aliens from East Africa increased as well. British Asians began arriving in the United Kingdom in growing numbers. This promoted the British Government to design and pass the Commonwealth Immigrants Act of 1968. While not the stated intent of the Act, it was clearly recognised by all parties in Britain that the new law was designed to retard, by the use of a quota system, the rate of entry of British Asians into the United Kingdom. Under the Immigrants Act of 1968, it became an offence for any citizen subject to immigration control to enter the country without being examined by immigration officers. In a review of the legal aspects of the expulsion order, Richard Plender noted:

> It is well known that the 1968 Act reduced the number of citizens of the United Kingdom and Colonies who might remain immune from immigration control. A citizen would enjoy this immunity only if he bore a United Kingdom passport and had been born, adopted, naturalised or registered in the United Kingdom.[16]

Most of the United Kingdom passport holders affected by the 1968 Commonwealth Immigrants Act, of course, were East African Asians. They could apply for employment vouchers like any other citizen of the Commonwealth; but, due to the magnitude and particular nature of their problem, 1,500 special entry vouchers were made available to these United Kingdom citizens each year. The quota of special vouchers was based on attempts to permit entry at rates similar to those years prior to the acceleration of immigration. It was argued that barring a serious deterioration of relationships between the East African Asians and the East African Governments or other untoward events, the quota was a fair one. Unfortunately, while the Asian situation in Kenya was stabilising, that in Uganda began deteriorating.

During the implementation of the 1968 Act, five categories of priorities were established for people waiting to enter the United Kingdom on special vouchers. In the top priority were those under notice to leave their country of residence by a certain date; the second category included persons barred from 'employment or trading' in their country of residence.[17] By late 1969, the first category alone was outstripping the availability of vouchers. While the pressure in category one dropped slightly in early 1970, the waiting list in category two almost doubled in size between January 31 and May 31 (2,150 to 3,800). The steady rise in the numbers on the waiting list (7,180 by May 31) in all categories was increasingly the result of a sharp rise in applications from Asians in Uganda.

The bulk of the backlog continued to be made up of Kenyan Asians, but by mid-1970, close to 2,000 Ugandan Asians were waiting for permission to enter Britain, and almost as many were awaiting preliminary interviews. Already many of those on the waiting lists were destitute, and the numbers who would be without financial resources would have increased by two-thirds by the end of 1971.[18] Clearly, the quota of special vouchers was nowhere near high enough to prevent an alarming increase in the number waiting to emigrate from East Africa to the United Kingdom and a similarly dramatic increase in the length of time Asians would have to wait for entry permission.

A safety valve of sorts was the arrangement made with the Government of India. Some British Asians in East Africa could have their passports endorsed for entry into India. This was done with the clear understanding that the ultimate responsibility for the immigrants would rest with Britain and the stay in India would be temporary. Another waiting list, composed of British Asians from East Africa waiting to enter the United Kingdom from India, thus was inaugurated.

The 1971 Immigration Act changed the common law right of entry to a statutory right of abode which was defined as applying to those persons with connections with the United Kingdom such that they qualify as patrials.[19] This produced a range of people with varying rights of entry: patrials, European Economic Community nations, Commonwealth nonpatrials, alien nonpatrials, and the Irish. In effect, the changes in the 1971 Act let in Australians, Canadians and New Zealanders, while it placed tight control on Commonwealth citizens from Africa and Asia. The patrials exemption specified that if a person's father were born in Britain, entry was permitted to that person. Many whites but few of other colours qualified under this rule. Nevertheless, it did leave three generations of whites liable to the same types of controls as the 'coloured citizens of the Commonwealth.'[20] In later policy adjustments, the chief exemption for Commonwealth citizens was extended to those who had either a father or a mother born in Britain. A person fitting this new patrial definition would be able to come and go and to work and settle in Britain without any restriction.

British immigration policies and the legal citizenship of the Ugandan Asians under international law were scrutinised closely as it became apparent that thousands of Asians would be coming to Britain. The fact that many Ugandan Asians have citizenship of the 'United Kingdom and colonies' (and no other citizenship) has certain consequences under international law, as Sir Peter Rawlinson, the Attorney General explained:

> A state is under duty to accept on its territory (in our case the United Kingdom or any dependency under United Kingdom sovereignty) those of its nationals who have nowhere else to go . . . . Thus if an Asian citizen of the United Kingdom and colonies is expelled from Uganda and is not accepted for settlement elsewhere, we can be required to accept him in any state where he then is.[21]

The legal obligation of Great Britain was reiterated in a television broadcast by Sir Alec Douglas-Home, Foreign and Commonwealth Secretary. He went on to speak of the great human problem and 'in the last resort, if homes elsewhere in the world cannot be found for them, we must take these unlucky people in.' He emphasised, 'They were already in great distress and anxiety, and the future for themselves and their property was uncertain. In some circumstances their lives could be in danger.'[22] The Shadow Home Secretary, Shirley Williams, speaking on radio several days later said: 'Britain has a clear obligation to offer a home to Asians from Uganda who hold British passports, but they should be encouraged to go to less crowded parts of the country.'[23] A *Times* editorial perhaps best put the situation in perspective on August 31:

> They trusted in the work of the British Government that they could come to Britain if life became intolerable for them where they were, and this right was even conceded by Mr Callaghan when as Home Secretary he was steering the restrictive Commonwealth Immigrants Bill through Parliament in 1968. If a man was thrown out of work and ejected from the country, he said, 'We shall have to take him. You cannot do anything else in these circumstances.' These are just the circumstances that have now arisen and it would be dishonourable and inhuman if Britain were now to leave in the

lurch those who had put their faith in an official British under-taking.[24]

The controversy over immigration was heightened by certain aspects of Britain's impending entry into the European Economic Community. One rule for participating members was unhindered entry for people seeking work. Of course, British workers could work elsewhere too. All fall, Great Britain moved ahead to meet its January 1, 1973 member-ship date even in the face of rising opposition. Procedural adjustments in the 1971 Immigration Act recommended for Parliamentary action did little to help 'whites' from Commonwealth countries to settle in Britain while 27,000 Asians or more were being taken at one time.[25]

The superimposition of two such emotional issues — Common Market membership and the admission of Ugandan Asian refugees — proved by mid-November to be too much of a strain for Conservative backbenchers and opposition members of Parliament. An unfavourable vote in the House of Commons on a Government-sponsored immigration measure was a jolting stab at the Government's immigration polices and Common Market plans. Although this did not topple the Government, given the procedural nature of the issue under discussion, it did bring immigration and Asian settlement questions to the forefront of national attention again.

Assuming the Burden

Despite the difficult times in the United Kingdom, the uneasiness of the British citizenry, the emotional attacks on the nation's immigration policy, and the Government's interpretation of it, there was little doubt that the Asians would be admitted. The mood in Britain, however, made it difficult for the Government to either announce its intentions to the public or implement a strategy to receive the Asians. Neverthe-less the Government steeled itself against further criticism and launched its preparations for the expellees.

Fortunately, not all of the news coming from Uganda and Britain was bad. At first it was difficult to get a clear definition of the parameters of the crisis. Slowly, as the days passed, a number of encouraging signs could be found. Each new development helped to settle the initial shock wave and to pave the way for acceptance of the refugees.

From the British viewpoint, the first good news was that the Indian High Commission in Uganda was granting entry visas to British Asians willing to recognise that they were the responsibility of Great Britain even though they could stay on a 'temporary' basis in India. This meant that between 10,000 and 15,000 might not be entering Britain immediately, and perhaps not at all. Many elderly people were reported to be in this group, people who did not want to adjust to the British climate and to another culture. Wealthy British Asians with property in India were also part of this group. Many professional people, businessmen and industrialists with resources outside Uganda, would, in all likelihood, go directly to India or to other countries after only a temporary stay in Britain.

The second encouraging sign was an announcement by Amin that noncitizen Asians in key managerial and technical positions would be allowed to remain in Uganda for at least twelve months. However, authorities estimated that this group consisted of only about 1,000 families, a relatively modest proportion of the noncitizen Asians in Uganda.

The third major news story was Canadian willingness to accept a large number of qualified Asians. That nation's immigration policy was based on a point system designed to evaluate whether a person would successfully adapt to the Canadian way of life. In order to gain admittance a person had to score 50 out of 100 points on such factors as education, fluency in either English or French, age, skills needed in the country, and family ties to Canadians. The key item to be underlined was that Canada had no colour barrier and no quotas on entry from particular areas or on specific nationalities. The commercial, skilled and white-collar background of the Ugandan Asians somewhat matched the needs of Canada. They would join 30,000 Indians and Pakistanis who had settled in Canada over the past five years. (As it turned out, over 7,000 Ugandan Asians were in Canada by the end of 1972.)[26]

In addition to India and Canada, five other countries were mentioned as being willing to offer help. New Zealand would take about 200; Sweden proposed to accept 200-300; and Malawi would take up to 1,000. Mauritius would accept expellees with certain professional qualifications and Bangladesh would take 'some' who would swear allegiance to the Bangladesh Government. A democratic congressman from New York asked the U.S. Government to allow 5,000 to enter the United States, although the American Government ultimately permitted only about 1,500 to immigrate. All these offers seemed to lighten, at least modestly, the burden the British would have to bear.

By the first of September, estimates of the total number of expelled Asians expected to arrive in Britain had dropped to 25,000-30,000. In addition to the decrease attributable to refugees going to other countries, groups registering in Kampala were averaging closer to three persons rather than the five that had been expected. Additionally, Whitehall was expressing confidence that the early arrivals would create few difficulties. They pointed out that the first group would consist primarily of those people who already had made plans for moving to Britain. It would be the next wave of the exodus for which definite preparation would be necessary.

Officials were becoming more confident of their ability to handle the situation because of reception efforts being organised by private groups. On 16 August, twenty national voluntary organisations met to form a coordinating committee to help the refugees and to promote their acceptance. On August 21, the British Council of Churches, already actively making contingency plans in cooperation with several groups, agreed to form a joint committee with the twenty voluntary organisations. This Coordinating Committee for the Welfare of Evacuees from Uganda represented a broad range of welfare, immigrant and charitable bodies. Among the sixty groups involved were the National Council of Social Service, the Community Relations Commission, Community Service Volunteers, the British Council of Churches Community and Race Relations Unit, Catholic Committee for Racial Justice, the Joint Council for the Welfare of Immigrants, the United Kingdom Immigrants Advisory Service, the Supreme Council of Sikhs in the United Kingdom, Oxfam Christian Action, and the Ismaili Community. A director, Miss Hannah Stanton, and a full-time staff were appointed immediately to begin meeting the needs of arriving Asians. During the height of the crisis, the Coordinating Committee's office was manned twenty-four hours a day, helping arrivals locate housing, furnishings, and employment.[27]

The Machinery of Response

As compared to typical governmental responses to movements of people from one area to another, the creation of the Uganda Resettlement Board, in mid-August, was an immense event. Normally immigration authorities expect that arrivals will find their own permanent abodes and generally secure their own futures. The URB, however, was given executive powers to organise the reception and resettlement of displaced United Kingdom passport holders from Uganda. The Board was to act as a liaison centre through which appropriate government departments, voluntary organisations, local authorities, and representatives of Asian immigrant groups could channel assistance to the newcomers. Almost from its inception, the Board was besieged by criticism. Its responsibilities and powers seemed 'vague,' complained the *Times*. Clearly, the positive impact of the Board would rest in its ability to 'induce action.'[28] On August 24, the appointment of Sir Charles Cunningham, a former permanent secretary at the Home Office, as the Board's chairman gave the liberal element in Britain little cause for rejoicing. Sir Charles, it would be remembered, was responsible for immigration in the 1950s, an administration which was considered by critics to have been overly concerned with maintaining the status quo. It appeared unlikely to these critics that the Board's leadership or its actions would be either aggressive or effective. One Asian, Praful Patel, a former resident of Uganda and the Secretary of the Committee on United Kingdom Citizenship, was named to the otherwise 'British' Board.[29]

After the first formal meeting of the Board on August 30, Sir Charles Cunningham announced three major priorities:

> To have arrangements ready to receive the families at the arrival points and to set up reception teams;
> To find temporary accommodations near arrival points for those who cannot go straight to their destinations.
> To try to persuade the arrivals to go to areas not under pressure in housing, education and social services.[30]

He mentioned two other priorities during his news conference: to help people find jobs, and to assess the impact of the new influx on local authority services. Cunningham went on to say:

> There are likely to be areas in which pressure on housing, schools, and the social services is already great. So we must do what we can to persuade immigrants — we cannot compel them to go elsewhere.[31]

As the Board machinery started to move into high gear, a number of significant actions were taken. Information was made available to Asians still in Uganda about the types of difficulties they might encounter in certain parts of the British Isles. Reception teams were drawn from various branches of the civil service and were installed at the major airports. A list of temporary accommodations began to grow daily, and a registry of employment offers started to take shape. An increase of contacts with local authorities across the country led to encouragement of dispersal. Finally, a charitable fund was organised to assist the Asians.

Later, in a step designed to bolster the Government's support of its Ugandan Asian policy, the Prime Minister, Mr Heath, announced that he was asking the Home Secretary, Mr Carr, to supervise arrangements for the settlement of Ugandan Asians in Great Britain. His responsibility was to coordinate the work of Whitehall departments assigned to resettle the new arrivals. In a radio interview, Mr Carr emphasised that he understood there was a strongly negative feeling in Britain toward coloured immigration but 'it has always been the British tradition that we honour our obligations.'[32] The statement by Mr Carr was in response to various alarming comments in the press such as those of Conservative MP, Mr Robert Redmond, Bolton West, who wrote to the

Prime Minister asking him to recall Parliament because he had 'never known such alarm in the country' and that the 'racialists were having a field day.'[33] A petition with 1,100 signatures objecting to further Asian immigration to Britain was presented to the Bolton Town Council. The *Local Government Chronicle* suggested that the Government adopt a population policy:

> Much of the hostility towards the arrival of the Asians stems not so much from racial or philistine attitudes, but from a genuine belief that this country is already overcrowded and that no really determined action is being taken to stop things getting worse.[34]

The Association of Municipal Corporations took an active role in asking the Government for assurances, 'as a matter of urgency,' that sufficient financial assistance would be forthcoming to communities receiving Ugandan Asians.[35] The question was whether the Board would go beyond mere acceptance responsibilities and actually work toward accommodation and absorption.

The Welcome Mat

The contributions of many groups at the airports, at resettlement centres, and in cities and villages across the land set examples of British conduct and commitment to help the oppressed. The shocking stories of families being driven from their Ugandan homes, robbed of their possessions, and beaten on the way to the airports came to light. Families arrived penniless in many cases. Most had to give up a comfortable way of life and attempt to start life anew. Some had been separated from loved ones in the movement out of Uganda. Stories of atrocities having been committed and of people having disappeared continued to make the news long after the Asians had departed. But perhaps the key factor in bringing the public to a greater level of tolerance and understanding during the fall of 1972 was General Amin's personal comparison of himself with Hitler. General Amin praised Adolf Hitler for his extermination campaign against the Jews:

> Germany is the right place where, when Hitler was Prime Minister and supreme commander, he burnt over 6 million Jews . . . . This is because Hitler and all German people knew that the Israelis are not people who are working in the interest of the people of the world and that is why they burnt the Israelis alive with gas in the soil of Germany.[36]

The reaction from around the world was one of extreme shock, anger, and outright condemnation. In Britain, people who previously had paid little attention to the Asians' plight in Uganda began to realise that here was a ruler of whom outrageous behaviour might be expected. Outright fear for the lives of Asians who were still trying to leave Uganda found greater expression among public and private leaders.

Time magazine summed up the reactions of many to Amin's analogy: 'Amin has established himself before the world as an ignorant, cruel and megalomaniacal despot.'[37] To merit this *Time* citation, Amin had not only made the statement about Hitler, but he had also investigated potential campsites for those Asians who would be interned after November 7. In addition, he charged that 'British crooks' were planning to assassinate him, and he put all 7,000 British personnel in Uganda under surveillance. Later, he expelled them, too. Among his utterances which found their way into the world press that week was a telegram from Amin to President Nyerere of Tanzania: 'I want to assure you that I love you very much, and if you had been a woman, I would have considered marrying you.'[38] Nyerere did not answer the telegram. The *Times* of Zambia put the problem in the most interesting perspective: 'Only in the befuddled mind of a punch-drunk ex-boxer could the fact be disputed that his operations against the Asians are giving Africa a bad name. God help the people of Uganda.'[39] Amin's statements during the months of the Asians' exodus were often quoted in the British press and were used appropriately in an attempt to ease the refugees' initial absorption.

To share a struggle with a people who had a Hitler type as their arch enemy was natural for a country which had fought so steadfastly against the onslaught of a fascist state. For many in the Women's Royal Voluntary Service, such desperately needed help had not been required since World War II. They travelled to old army camps and air force bases to help thousands of Asians settle into temporary quarters; they put together the necessary bedding and clothing; and they offered comfort and services to an appreciative group of newcomers. In the seesaw battle between British justice and British racialism, Amin's cruel ramblings and responses such as those of the Women's Royal Voluntary Service clearly aided the Asians' cause. In addition, the predominance of pro-Asian elements in the reception process would serve to promote the Asians' progress towards absorption.

The reputed middle-class background of the Ugandan Asians and their desirable occupational skills were dominant themes of the press. British newspapers helped relate the sensitive story of intelligent human beings, forced to move from their country and to settle on a 'tiny island' which was not sure it had room for them. The 'liberal' press played a crucial role in the autumn of 1972 unfolding of this migration. In an article entitled 'Arriving for the Jobs We Won't Take,' the London *Evening Standard*, for example, attempted to assuage one of the Britishers' fears — job competition from the Asians. The story discussed the advantages of having this 'relatively small coloured work force of perhaps 15,000 people' in the industrial sections of Great Britain, particularly the Midlands. Two decades of full employment had given tens of thousands of workers the opportunity to advance up the socio-economic ladder. According to the *Evening Standard,* this had created a 'manpower gap' throughout industry. There were 900,000 unemployed, but they would no longer work at 'any job.' Openings in London Transport for 2,167 bus drivers, 994 conductors, and 290 tube station staff were vacant largely because most people were seeking higher paid jobs. Positions with textile firms, skilled trade groups and computer programming slots were in demand among others. The *Evening Standard* was quite frank as to why the foundries in the Midlands, for example, were staffed in large measure by Asians:

> The answer to those who play the 'numbers game,' that because unemployment is steadily more than 800,000 — around the same level as the immigrant work force — this means that white and coloured workers are in competition with each other for jobs, is that British workers often do not want many of the dirty and heavy jobs now being done by immigrants.[40]

The media, and particularly television, attempted to forge a close link between the Asians' basically British way of life in East Africa and the social milieu of Britain. As suggested in one analysis: 'It is likely that they have more potential for coming to terms with life in Britain than many of their predecessors. But the way their occupational and cultural position has been described suggests a felt need to present them as such in order to facilitate acceptance of the decision to admit them.'[41] The 'numbers game' began to settle down, and people became less frightened that their particular piece of real estate was going to be overrun. The governmental machinery regeared in early November from setting the tone of the British welcome to processing people through the resettlement camps. The focus shifted to guiding people toward permanent homes, job opportunities and a new way of life. Many would find communities welcoming them openly. Many would find that they were not only welcome but needed. All would find a multi-racial society beginning to look in the mirror.

Notes

1. The London *Sunday Telegraph*, August 6, 1972.
2. The *Times*, September 13, 1972.
3. *Ibid.*
4. The *Times*, September 8, 1972.
5. The migrations were called 'the most spectacular migration of human beings of which history has yet had record' and were 'accomplished in the face of official indifference and sometimes hostility.' W. Churchill, *The Great*

Democracies, Vol. IV of *A History of the English Speaking People* (New York, 1958), pp. 98-99.

6. For pre-1970 figures, see E.J.B. Rose, *et al.* in *Colour and Citizenship* (London, 1969), p. 99. For 1971 figures see *1971 Census, Great Britain, Advance Analysis*, Table 2, (HMSO, 1972).

7. *The Guardian Weekly*, August 19, 1972, p. 7.

8. A wealth of sources are available on the history of the British Empire. The most comprehensive is *The Cambridge History of the British Empire*. Other general references consulted include: C. Cross, *The Fall of the British Empire* (London, 1968); G. Graham, *A Concise History of the British Empire* (New York, 1970); W.K. Hancock, *The Wealth of Colonies* (London, 1940); P. Knaplund, *The British Empire 1815-1939* (New York, 1941); E.A. Walker, *The British Empire: Its Structures and Spirit* (2nd edn, London, 1953); J.A. Williamson, *A Short History of British Expansion* (2 vols, London, 1964). A useful reference specific to the empire in Africa is: J.R. Robinson and J. Gallagher, *Africa and the Victorians* (London, 1961).

9. 'Like Topsy [the empire] just growed.' Knaplund, *op. cit.*, p. xviii.

10. One author suggested this reason: 'The British were industrial colonists on their own earth,' and thus had 'little time' for thoughts on overseas possessions. H. Bolitho (ed.), *The British Empire* (London, 1947), p. 5.

11. Knaplund, *loc. cit.*

12. Shiva Naipaul in a newspaper account on the refugees states that their colonial dependence had produced 'a sort of mental paralysis' in the East African Asians. 'We always knew that one day we would have to come,' *The Sunday Times Magazine*, December 31, 1972, p. 27.

13. Elspeth Huxley, 'England faces the Great Migration,' *National Review*, October 13, 1972, p. 1124.

14. Iain Macleod, letter to the *Spectator,* February 23, 1968.

15. Y. Tandon, 'A Political Survey' in D. Ghai and Y. Ghai (eds), *Portrait of a Minority* (Nairobi, 1970), p. 96

16. Richard Plender, 'The Expulsion of the Asians from Uganda; Legal Aspects,' *New Community*, Vol. I, No. 5, p. 421.

17. The other categories of priority: (3) Persons unable to find employment; (4) others wishing to emigrate.

18. Over 3,600 in Uganda alone. Estimate of J.C.W.I. as presented to Select Committee on Race Relations and Immigration (Evidence, pp. 858-70).

19. Part I, Immigration Act 1971, Chapter 77 (HMSO, 1971).

20. For a discussion of this dimension of the Act, see the *Bulletin* of the Runnymede Trust, February and March, 1973.

21. As quoted in the *Times*, September 9, 1972.

22. The *Times*, September 1, 1972.

23. As quoted in Douglas Tilbe, *The Ugandan Asian Crisis* (London, 1972), p. 10.

24. The *Times*, August 31, 1972.

25. Implication of these actions are discussed in the *Bulletin* of the Runnymede Trust for January, February and March, 1973.

26. The *Times*, September 5, 1972.

27. Personal interviews with Hannah Stanton and Coordinating Committee Staff, December, 1972.

28. The *Times*, August 19, 1972.

29. To the extent that a look at the levels of officials recruited for service on the Board is useful, the following is noted. In addition to Cunningham and Patel, other members of the Board were Mark Bonham Carter, Chairman of the Community Relations Commission; Mrs Charles Clode, Chairman of the

Women's Royal Voluntary Service; Mr B. Wilson, Town Clerk of the London borough of Camden; Sir Walter Coutts, an ex-Governor General of Uganda; Sir Ronald Ironmonger, Leader of the Sheffield City Council; Sir Frank Marshall of the Leeds City Council; Lord Thorneycroft, and Douglas Tilbe, Director of the Community and Race Relations Unit of the British Council of Churches.

30. The *Times*, August 31, 1972.
31. *Ibid.*
32. Quoted in the *Times*, September 4, 1972.
33. The *Times*, September 2, 1972.
34. Quoted in the *Guardian*, September 21, 1972.
35. *Ibid.*
36. 'God Help the People,' *Time*, September 25, 1972.
37. *Ibid.*
38. *Ibid.*
39. *Ibid.*
40. *London Evening Standard*, August 31, 1972.
41. Robin H. Ward, 'The Decision to Admit,' *New Community*, Vol. I, No. 5, Autumn 1972, p. 433.

4. RESETTLEMENT CENTRES: RECEPTION AND RELOCATION

Rambhai Patel (a pseudonym) was the last person in the long queue for dinner at the Greenham Common Resettlement Centre dining hall. He rubbed his hands in the chill of an early January evening. Mr Patel was one of 1,700 Ugandan Asians at this Centre, located within the confines of a United States Air Force Base an hour west of London. Filling his tray with Indian food, he walked across the noisy dining hall to join his mother, his wife, and four of their five children, ranging in age from 5 to 18. The fifth child had been out of Uganda for over a year before the crisis, studying microbiology and chemistry in California. Mr Patel was 48 years old and his wife, about three or four years younger. She smiled broadly, nodding her head, but she did not understand much English. She was taking language classes at the Centre in order to become acquainted with the vocabulary necessary to buy food and goods in their new country. He spoke to her in Gujerati as he did to his mother who ate quietly attending to the children. The children had no difficulty with English, conversing in that language among themselves and with two volunteer workers seated at the same table. Mr Patel, also competent in English, discussed his plight with the volunteers: how he had built a life for his family in Uganda and then had suddenly found his world collapsing around him, forcing him to bring his whole family to a wintry resettlement camp on a military base in England. Mr Patel related that he migrated to Uganda in 1950 to start a new life. He recalled that his grandfather had gone to East Africa during the construction of the railroad at the turn of the century but had later returned to his family in Gujerat. Following his grandfather's example, Mr Patel had moved to East Africa in order to improve his economic lot. He, unlike his grandfather, had decided to stay, and after a year in Uganda, sent for his family. For the past fifteen years, Mr Patel had been manager of a British firm offering mechanical and technical engineering services in Kampala. He had owned a home and had driven a Volkswagen. Mr Patel commented: 'We were enjoying our home, the sunshine, food and vegetables. We really made our home in Uganda, and we feel that we have really been uprooted. We are like Robinson Crusoe.' Discussion about how the children were taking the shock of leaving their country at such short notice and having little hope of ever returning, caused Mr Patel to smile, and then he said thoughtfully,

Yes, it was quite a shock, you know. But the children are feeling a bit of adventure. They have the shelter of a mother and father in starting a new life. Yes, it is really difficult for them, but then again they are a bit happy to see a new world. I am sure they will be adjusting themselves sooner than what we adults can do.

Regarding what they had been able to take with them from Uganda, Mr Patel lamented that they had been able to salvage only a fraction of the things they owned. 'Most of the things we had to discard for almost nothing,' he said, shaking his head in disbelief at his own words. 'All our money is still in the bank there, and we can't get it out.' They were able to take £50 with them when they hurriedly departed from Entebbe Airport in the British-arranged airlift to England.

One of the volunteers mentioned the shipping crates and luggage marked with United Kingdom destinations that was stacked in the entry way of the administration building. It reminded the Patels of the tons of Asian possessions left behind at Entebbe Airport. Unaccompanied baggage was piled in the open air, and much was lost due to pilfering or weather. Large quantities that did reach England had lost all identification, and the process to determine proper ownership was a slow one. Like the Patels, many of the Asian families were left with only what they had been able to carry aboard the chartered flights. The Patels had not been separated, and that was one relief among many fears. They had read in the Kampala newspaper, the *Argus*, that many British were upset about the sudden influx of Asians, and the Patels did not know how they would be received or what would happen to them.

Clutching their British passports as they arrived at London's Heathrow Airport, they were pleased but bewildered, Mr Patel recalled, by all the officials and volunteers there to greet them and to usher them in for a hot meal after the long journey. 'Of course,' Rambhai Patel commented, sipping his tea as the dining hall began to clear, 'we had never given up our British passports, so we hoped we would be eligible for help upon arrival, and we were.' Amid all of the confusion and weariness of the trip, he was pleased with a cover from the British *Economist* magazine a British volunteer had tacked on the camp bulletin board:

WELCOME
British Passport Holders

We know many of you didn't really want to leave your homes and jobs in Uganda.
You know we didn't really want you to come before because we have problems with homes and jobs here.

But most of us believe that this is a country that can use your
skills and energies.
We have worked out plans about how you should start and where you
should go. They won't be perfect but they will help.
You will find that we, like other countries, have our bullies and misfits.
We are particularly sorry about those of our politicians who are trying
to use your troubles for their own ends.
And we're glad your British passport means something again.[1]

Several people even wrote home that first night to relatives still in
Uganda saying: 'It's all right; you can come to Great Britain. They do
welcome you, and they say they will help you find accommodations
and work.'

The reception teams processing the Patel family and others at the
airport were those formed by the Uganda Resettlement Board. A host
of volunteer organisations at the airports and at the camps helped to
ease the transition. Mr Patel and his family were housed at a transit
centre, Kensington, in central London. With no acquaintances in
England to assist them, the Patels were unable to locate employment or
housing. After a few days, they were transferred to Greenham Common,
a larger centre capable of handling people for a more extended period
and of offering them the type of resettlement assistance they would
require.

Opening of the 'Transit Camps'

Earlier convictions had been that, if necessary at all, the resettlement
centres would be for one- or two-day transit stops before Asians made
their way into the British communities. The centres were indeed
necessary, and they soon took on a very different character. It had been
anticipated that certainly the early arrivals would be largely self-sufficient.
Some had arrived prior to the airlift and before the centres began
functioning. Through friends and relatives and with the help of volunteer
organisations, they had made their way into the community. But the
very first 'immigrant flight' gave indications of a substantial need which
the centres would have to serve. Of the 193 passengers on that first
plane, 101 had no place to go upon arrival.[2] Fortunately, signals from
the interviews in Uganda had alerted the Board to this situation. The
refugees were taken to Stradishall, the first 'transit camp' to open.

The arriving Asians were to be housed almost entirely on disused
military installations. For example, Stradishall near Newmarket in
Suffolk was an ex-Royal Air Force Base, which had not been used for
two years. As military bases typically are, these bases were scattered
around the country, some in rather isolated locations.

62

By October 1, nearly 3,000 out of the 4,000 refugees who had arrived were in three of what were still regarded as transit camps.[3] By the time Rambhai Patel and his family arrived in late October, he recalled few expellees being met by relatives; instead most were going to camps. This unanticipated dependency alarmed the Resettlement Board. Why had such a large percentage of Asians needed the camps in the first place, and why were they leaving at such a slow rate?

The Asians' inability to find their own way was particularly puzzling to British officials because these early arriving families, as noted above, had been on the waiting list to enter Britain. Many had contacts in the United Kingdom. One explanation stemmed from the nature of the immigration. Typically, a head-of-household migrating to Britain would make the initial move from East Africa and be followed later by his dependents. In such cases, friends or relatives in the United Kingdom could easily accommodate the new immigrant, even if he were accompanied by another wage-earning member of the family. The forced migration from Uganda allowed no such luxury of convenience.[4]

Whole families, and often extended family units, such as the Patel family, arrived together. Few friends or relatives had space in their homes to accept such a substantial influx. Additionally, most of the refugees arrived destitute of funds and would have been unable to afford housing even if it had been available. One told a newsman, 'Actually, I was going to come [to England] earlier. The only difference is that then I would have had some money, and now I am penniless.'[5]

The slow rate of leaving the centres was attributable in part to the policy, formulated by the Department of Employment and Productivity, that obtaining a job was the highest priority for the refugee. That this was an unworkable plan quickly became obvious. The Resettlement Board quietly abandoned its initial policy of matching jobs with homes and began to concentrate on finding homes for the Asians.

An even more immediate need was for emergency accommodations. At the height of the airlift, thousands of Asians were arriving each week. Stradishall quickly reached saturation and proved that, while it could be pleasant with 800 occupants, conditions were almost intolerable with 1,600. Other military installations were hurriedly pressed into service.

The United States offered to allow portions of their standby base at Greenham Common to be used as a reception centre. The Board accepted, and 1,700 Asians were sent there. Air Force officers said the number the base could accommodate was flexible, but probably was up to twice as many as the URB intended to house there.[6] Buildings, which Asian families such as the Patels occupied, had been unused for at least three years, but they had been maintained in the event of a military emergency. Greenham Common proved to be a most useful and versatile operation. In addition to acting as a transit centre from which Asians were assigned to other camps, it developed an active resettlement programme for its own tenants. Later, it housed all of the stateless Asians who had illegally entered Britain during the crisis and thus were under detention.

Eventually, sixteen resettlement centres and transit camps were opened by the URB. The selections made for camps or centres were, sometimes, unfortunate. Several centres had what were, at best, marginal facilities. Some were fire hazards, others extremely difficult to maintain. One was located in a particularly harsh climatic environment. These problems caused certain centres to be closed even before others had opened.

The shutting down of any centre and the resulting movement of its residents created a measure of apprehension among the Asians. Critics of the URB suggested that such actions were another sign of the Board's lack of sensitivity to the human side of the crisis. As the number of refugees in the centres later declined, the closing of some centres was, of course, a logical economic step. Mr Carr had estimated in October '. . . that the camps are costing us about £1 million a month to run all in . . .'[7] The decision to close a centre for whatever reasons was never a popular one with the refugees, centre staff or volunteer workers.

One such case hit the British press at Christmas time and aroused indignation about the Board's activities. The centre at Hobbs Barracks was closing due to 'unacceptable' fire risks in the wooden barracks. After complaints about the inhumanity of moving people over the Christmas season, the transfer was delayed until after 1 January. One hundred and twenty-one of these refugees went to Maresfield Centre which itself closed just over a month later. The transfers generally were handled in good style, and the receiving centres did as much as possible to make the change an easy one for the Asians. Still, it was disruptive and tended to retard the work toward resettlement.[8]

At Greenham Common, with no knowledge of what the next day would bring in terms of opportunities to find suitable accommodation and employment to support their family, the six Patels had found comfort from residence in an Asian community, no matter how ephemeral. Their living at the Centre provided a measure of security, but it meant they still faced the task of confronting the British community.

Mr Patel observed, 'Very frankly speaking, we have not yet come into contact with the British way of life. You know, we are still gathered into the flock which came from Uganda.' The Patels, however, were not as divorced from the British life ways as were families at many of the other centres. Because of its location close to London, the scope of its operation, its obvious interest for Americans, and a camp administrator

64

who realised the value of publicity, Greenham entertained numerous visitors, both official and unofficial.

The Patel family could have just as well have been sent to the other end of the 'isolation spectrum' such as the centre at Tonfanau, on the coast in west-central Wales. Six hours to London by train and a considerable distance to the nearest community of any size, its isolation was impressive. Locations such as that of Tonfanau prompted additional criticism of the Board. Lord Hawke, speaking in the House of Lords, put it this way:

> These Ugandan Asians are extremely capable people. After all, they ran Uganda; and, given half a chance, they will soon establish themselves in this country, and within a generation or two they may be running this country. But they cannot do it from these remote camps; and I was astonished when I saw that the Government were popping these people into remote areas of the country. I do not quite know why. If only they could find camps somewhere near where the jobs are, these people would soon find jobs.[9]

Many of the Asians had similar feelings about being so far removed from the great urban areas where almost all would eventually live and work. The Ugandan Ismailis were directed by their leaders in the United Kingdom not to accept accommodation at a centre more than sixty miles from London.

Was there, in fact, a strategy behind the selection of certain bases? Did the URB view the locations of the camps as part of the grand design to disperse Asians widely in Britain? Government officials denied that they were.[10] The choice of bases generally seemed to relate more to practical considerations such as condition and availability. If such a strategy did exist, either consciously or subconsciously, its success was to be minimal.

Over half of these Asians, like the Patel family still in the centres in January, would depend completely on the resettlement office for relocation in Britain. This was the group on which the resettlement officers were concentrating. Few of the families offered the degree of challenge to relocation as that of a particular Muslim family in which the head-of-household was stateless and in a refugee camp in Europe, while his two wives and thirteen other dependents were at Greenham Common. Many of the families, however, did have special needs brought about by separation from the heads-of-household, illness, schooling requirements, or in some cases, sheer size. Resettlement officers paid special attention to relocating these families in an attempt to ensure that as the months passed, the Asians remaining in the centres would not be only 'hard care' problem cases.[11]

As the stay in the camps became lengthy for some families, a provocative question arose: were the Asians becoming reluctant to leave the relative comfort and security offered by some of the centres? The senior regional camp commandant for the south-west, suggesting it was a 'very serious problem,' put it this way:

> What happens is that you make the place into an extremely comfortable camp. [The Asians] are warm, well fed, given pocket money by social security. TV and that sort of thing is provided. You are reducing the incentive for them to get out into the big wide world, for the camp must represent security for them.[12]

The resettlement staff at Greenham Common was not in total accord. Responding to a question about the Asians' developing a false sense of security in the centres, the senior resettlement officer replied: 'A very small percentage may. The vast majority have accepted the situation. They realise the sooner they go out into Britain, the better.'[13] The Patel family had agreed unanimously with this conclusion. They had accepted an offer of Council housing in the north-west of England despite no immediate hope of employment for any of the family.

Baroness Eirene White put it more strongly: 'I must say that in my own visits to camps, I've been tremendously impressed by the eagerness of everybody there to get out of the camps into normal life and to make a new start.' Lady White also noted 'the frustration which many of [the Asians] feel, because the arrangements for jobs and houses are taking, in some instances, a very long time,' and concluded that 'the proportion who would really want to go on in that kind of life must be very small indeed.'[14] Her statement would later be proven as an accurate assessment.

For that small proportion, however, the lengthening period in the centres served to emphasise any reluctance to relocate in the United Kingdom.

Operation of the 'Resettlement Centres'

As the statutory body responsible for the Asians on their arrival in Britain, the URB had to deal with many aspects of the immigration. The Board's contact with many of the refugees would be minimal, and a good deal of the work of receiving the Asians would be done by voluntary organisations beyond its jurisdiction. Yet, it would be the URB which would be held ultimately accountable for the success or failure of the 'resettlement' process.

The Director of the Board was in charge of its day-to-day operations, and bearing the brunt of the Board's work were its Divisions Three and Four.[15] Division Three was responsible for the administration of resettlement centres, while Four was responsible for the resettlement teams at those centres. This dichotomy was retained at the individual centre level where it was to create some difficulties resulting from philosophical differences over the centres' functions.

Most of the camp administrators and their deputies were former military officers, whose names were found on Britain's roster of executives available for employment. A number of these men, in addition to having the obvious advantage, from the Board's perspective, of being familiar with military installations, also had experience in East Africa. One, for example, had been a District Officer in Kenya. Another had served in the military in East Africa, and a third had been a prison officer. The camp administrators were responsible for the logistics of the centres — lodging, food, transportation, and working with the voluntary organisations providing services to the Asians.

The administrators had little authority with which to carry out their responsibilities. Problems continually arose concerning sanitation, fire hazards, and Asians not meeting commitments. In addition to persuasion and what one camp administrator referred to in an interview as 'constant nagging,' the withdrawal of some of the already modest privileges of the Asians was employed to encourage conformity to camp standards.[16] For example, one of the most sensitive logistical issues facing the administrators, and the one that may have given more trouble than any other, was food. The refugees were fed in the military mess halls, which never have been known to foster healthy appetites or good digestion. The meals were prepared by catering services and typically offered a choice of English or Asian fare. No single Asian menu could satisfy the variety of ethnic, religious and geographic culinary preferences found among the refugees. But occasional insensitivities produced unnecessary problems. At Greenham Common, separate food lines for Asian and English food created the impression of a gastronomic apartheid. A hunger strike was threatened by the Asians, but it never materialised.[17]

The work of voluntary organisations was crucial in opening up the resettlement centres and later in performing many valuable services in their operation. For example, at Greenham Common Centre, which was set up in a period of just over two weeks, Women's Royal Voluntary Service (WRVS), the Red Cross, and St John Ambulance were active. Additionally, work was done 'above all by voluntary workers in the local parishes who have been encouraged to come and work by the Salvation Army who have been tremendously helpful here.'[18]

The WRVS played the major role in aiding government officials in opening and equipping centres. Because of the nature of their activities (e.g. preparing the quarters, providing bedding and clothing), the WRVS people were seldom in conflict with the camp administrator. The organisations of the Coordinating Committee concerned more with such aspects as social well-being, education, entertainment were in some cases at odds with the centre administration. This appeared to be particularly true of the organisations which had young volunteers. The enthusiastic workers interpreted centre administration's conservatism regarding the provision of certain types of camp facilities as a sign of disinterest in the plight of the refugees. A minor controversy, for example, had arisen at Doniford Centre, regarding the establishment of a shop to sell sundries to the refugees.[19] Young volunteers ran foul of regulations and found themselves in sharp disagreement with the camp administrator. Some of the volunteers accused the Government of providing nothing at the centre beyond quarters and food service. While this charge, undoubtedly spurred by the degree of frustration felt by the volunteers, was not true, their concern about the lack of recreational facilities was a valid one, and not only at Doniford.

The nature of the activities of the volunteer organisations, particularly those of the Coordinating Committee, and disagreements over what facilities the Government should provide, point up the not-always-happy relationship the volunteers had with camp administrators. A number of administrators pointed to problems they were having with the Coordinating Committee people. Some suggested that they had to guard against the Committee's taking over responsibilities and authority which were clearly in the purview of the statutory bodies. It is difficult to evaluate the effect these disagreements had on the functioning of the centres, but it certainly created difficulties for the administrators and disillusionment among some of the volunteers.

How did the Asians get along with the administration in the centres? Two aspects of this question seemed particularly intriguing. One was the potential problem created by the variety of religious and sectarian groupings the Asians brought with them from East Africa. A second was the potential hostility fostered by the political and military conflicts in the early 1970s on the Indian subcontinent.

The effects created by the latter situation appeared to be minimal. While sensitivities did exist between Hindu and Muslim, they tended to be religious rather than political in nature. Camp administrators, sensitive to the potential difficulty, took steps to avoid any serious confrontations. At Greenham Common, for example, the administrator made certain that if the chairman of his Asian advisory committee (composed of refugees) was a Muslim, the deputy chairman was a Hindu.[20] Of all the Asian communities which migrated to Britain, one in particular gave the resettlement centre administrators difficulty. The Ismaili community, as efficiently organised in Britain as it had been in Uganda, checked carefully on the treatment its members were receiving in the centres. Ismaili leaders continually visited the centres, giving assistance and advice to Ismailis living there. If the advice given to them from the community was in conflict with instructions from the centre officials, the Ismailis would disobey the officials. It was reported that not only did they attempt to gain control of the camp committees, but they also sought special treatment from the administration. At Maresfield Centre, the situation became so tense that the Ismailis were split up and sent to other camps.[21]

In general, camp administrators and other centre staff had high praise for the good spirit, adaptability, and peacefulness of the Asians. Despite crowded conditions, various cultural backgrounds and considerable uncertainty as to the future, the interpersonal difficulties among the Asians were minimal.

From Camp to Community

Each of the camps was assigned a resettlement officer, whose job included coordinating the work of the different departments concerned with relocating the Asians. These men were senior civil servants on loan from various governmental units, and they answered directly to the head of the Resettlement Division in URB headquarters, London.

They began their work in early October, after the URB had recognised that the 'transit camps' would have to become, in most cases, 'resettlement centres.' The senior resettlement officers at each centre began to assemble staff, set up record keeping, and develop a strategy for handling the basic job of relocating the Asians.

The official relationship of senior resettlement officer to camp administrator was an interesting one. As noted earlier, the logistical and resettlement functions were kept separate at both URB headquarters and the centres. While this did present some difficulties in decision-making at the centres,[22] the dichotomy did offer one potential advantage: the resettlement staff could remain aloof from the difficulties and disputes which arose between Asians and the centre administration. Without doubt, this permitted a happier relationship between Asian refugees and resettlement officers.

The Resettlement Board allowed such a degree of local autonomy in the resettlement offices that no single mode of operation emerged. It is true, however, that despite variations from one senior resettlement officer to another, a basic philosophy pragmatically evolved out of early difficulties. As noted above, the early resettlement strategy was to match man, job, and accommodation. After it readily became apparent that this was a totally unrealistic goal, the major task of the resettlement scheme became one of locating residences for the families.

Employment, while certainly a matter of concern, did not retain the priority in resettlement thinking that it had initially held. This resulted from two basic concepts. First, while employment in some locations was difficult to find, housing was an even more pressing problem in Britain. Second, previous East African Asian immigrants often had been able to obtain work in Britain, even in areas of relatively high unemployment.

Unfortunately, employment was to prove a very real problem for many of the Asians. The refugees were not going to make the transition from work in Uganda to work in the United Kingdom as easily as the URB was hoping.

This fact could have been anticipated. Information reaching Britain from the High Commission in Uganda during the early days of the crisis confirmed a very high rate of self-employment among the Asians. The qualifications of people within the category ranged widely and often were difficult to define. Propaganda circulated by Asian leaders in Britain made the employment matter more complex. Attempting to counter opposition to admission of the Asians to Britain, the refugees who were to arrive from Uganda were described as all being well-educated and competent in English. Some of the illusions of the resettlement workers were soon to be shattered. Although the young showed the results of European-style schooling, many people of older generations could speak little or no English. Even the early arrivals did not all speak English, and the situation worsened as the second wave of immigrants arrived.

While this created immediate problems in the processing and in the temporary housing of the refugees, it would prove more serious as a handicap to finding a suitable job. Department of Employment figures suggest that as of 1 January, 20-25 per cent of those seeking work needed English language training. Small wonder that one of the major priorities of volunteer organisations aiding the refugees after they were relocated was for establishment of English classes, particularly for heads-of-households seeking employment. Language acculturation was not as widespread as had been anticipated.

Of the first 1,500 Asians interviewed by Department of Employment personnel at the resettlement centres, 6 per cent were professional people, 33 per cent were commercial and clerical workers, 25 per cent were skilled, 36 per cent semi-skilled, and 12 per cent unskilled. Most of these were heads-of-households who had planned to emigrate from Uganda to Britain, irrespective of Amin's decree.[23]

In addition, the discrepancies between the previous occupation in Uganda (as stated by the immigrant) and the job suggested by the Department of Employment interviewers were substantial. At Doniford Resettlement Centre, for example, only 21 per cent of those registered with the Employment office retained their Uganda job classification, and one out of every three interviewed at the Centre was designated for unskilled factory work. Many of those had been self-employed in Uganda.[24]

Considerable numbers of housewives were registering with the Employment Office. The unsettled nature of their situation, plus the physical separation from husband and/or family, required that more women seek employment than would have been the case in Uganda. While the younger women may have been trained and employed while still in Uganda, due to traditional roles, housewives seldom were. Most housewives who sought employment consequently were qualified only as domestic servants or as unskilled factory workers. The presence of previously unemployed women in the employment lists clearly accounts for some of the apparent differences in job skill levels between the early and later arrivals. Although the expectations of the British officials regarding the Asians' employment potential were not always met, it would be misleading to assume that most of the immigrants were unemployable. Such was not the case. Many of those having difficulty finding suitable work were not willing immediately to accept jobs well below the level of employment for which they felt qualified.

As the weeks passed, resettlement officers were feeling pressure from the Board to expedite the Asians' departures from the centres. Whether it was justified or not, some resettlement officers did come under criticism for the amount of pressure that they, in turn, were applying to Asian heads-of-household to accept offers of job and/or housing. Such officers, it was claimed, were more interested in good departure statistics than in good resettlement.

Basically, the strategy proceeded in this fashion. If a head-of-house-hold was offered a job, he or she was encouraged to take the job, find temporary accommodation in the community, and if necessary, leave the family in the centre until more permanent housing was found. The resettlement officers claimed that the breadwinner, already out in the community, was in a good position to locate more permanent housing for his or her family. In some cases, the head-of-household refused to take up a job offer if it meant leaving the family behind. Even if the Department of Employment had located the job, it was in no position to force acceptance of that job.

If housing were located for a family by the resettlement officers, but if no job were immediately available, the resettlement people were more insistent on the family leaving the centre. Of course, they, like the Department of Employment, could not force the people to accept the housing, but they tried diligently to convince the family to do so. With proper housing, the family, it was suggested, could maintain themselves through social security benefits even if the wage earner were not employed.

Both approaches appeared to be logical ones. A wage earner out in the community in which he hoped to reside would have a good chance to consider the full range of housing possibilities open in that area. On the other hand, if housing were available in a town or city, but the Department of Employment had no job listing in that location, it was still possible work could be obtained once the family was settled. It is estimated that only one-fifth of job vacancies ever appeared on the official listing.

So, through the efforts of resettlement officers or without any assistance at all, the Asian families steadily, if not rapidly, were leaving the centres. In accepting jobs and housing, they began the elaboration of their social sphere beyond that confined social grouping of the centre and the refugee community; they took the first steps in the development of new roles and identities in British society. The resettlement staff, as carefully as possible, recorded every family's new address and, if appropriate, notified the local authority of the arrival of the immigrants.

Notes

1. *The Economist*, August 19, 1972.
2. Data obtained from URB.
3. From URB weekly status reports.
4. A comparison of immigration statistics for 1971 and 1972 emphasises this point. In 1971 2,956 special voucher holders and 7,732 dependents arrived in the United Kingdom. In 1972 these figures were 3,260 and 23,129 respectively. From *Control of Immigration Statistics, 1972*, HMSO (1973).
5. *Time*, October 30, 1972, p. 43.
6. Personal interviews, Greenham Common, January 17, 1973.
7. Parliamentary debates, House of Commons, October 18, 1972.
8. Personal interviews, Maresfield Centre, December 28-29, 1972 and January 20 and 23, 1973.
9. Parliamentary debates, House of Lords, December 6, 1972.
10. For example, Mr Eldon Griffiths, Parliamentary Under Secretary of State at the Department of Environment in press conference, Stradishall, September 8, 1972.
11. Personal interview, Mr I. Rosser, Senior Resettlement Officer, Tonfanau Resettlement Centre, January 5, 1973.
12. *Uganda Argus*, October 30, 1972. The Ugandan newspapers were carefully following the arrival of the Asians in Britain.
13. Personal interview, Mr Eric Bailey, Greenham Common, January 24, 1973.
14. Personal interview, London, January 25, 1973.
15. Mr T.A. Critchley, an Assistant Under Secretary of State in the Home Office, was appointed the Board's Director.
16. Personal interviews, Maresfield Centre, December 29, 1972.
17. Personal interviews, Greenham Common, January 17-18, 1973.
18. Personal interview, Brigadier G.H.B. Beyts, Greenham Common, January 24, 1973.
19. Personal interviews, Doniford Centre, January 1973.
20. Personal interview, Brigadier G.H.B. Beyts, Greenham Common, January 15, 1973.
21. Personal interviews, S.E. Bussey, Maresfield Resettlement Centre, December 28, 1972.

22. For example, in the matter of responsibility for transportation of Asians to look at places of potential residence or employment.
23. Department of Employment and Productivity data as presented at Friends House, London, January 6, 1973.
24. From Department of Employment and Productivity records, Doniford Resettlement Centre, January 1973.

5. THE DISPERSAL OF THE IMMIGRANTS: RED AREAS AND GREEN AREAS

From interviews with Asians in Kampala early in the crisis, a disturbing fact had begun to appear. Most intended to go to those areas of Britain which, in the opinion of many authorities, would have the greatest difficulty in absorbing them. For example, one out of every four groups was headed for Leicester. That East Midlands city has one of the largest concentrations of East African Asians in the United Kingdom outside of London itself. Council leaders, pointing to the 7,000 unemployed in the city and to the strain a major Asian influx would place on housing and on the Leicester schools, took matters into their own hands. The Council purchased in a Kampala paper a half-page advertisement urging expelled Asians not to settle in Leicester. The ad boldly proclaimed:

> IN THE INTEREST OF YOURSELF AND YOUR FAMILY, YOU SHOULD ACCEPT THE ADVICE OF THE UGANDA RESETTLE-MENT BOARD AND NOT COME TO LEICESTER.[1]

The Strategy of Relocation

The URB 'advice' to which the advertisement alluded was part of the Board's most controversial plan. It decided to designate certain areas of Britain as ones to which the Asians would be dissuaded from going, others as ones to which they would be encouraged to go.

Four social and economic conditions of an area were considered in the decision to designate it 'red' or undesirable for a large Asian influx: housing, schools, social services, and employment. If the area were in severe difficulty in two or more of these aspects, it was believed necessary to discourage Asian immigrants from settling there, and thus it was labelled a 'red area.' In every case, this included severe pressure on the social services, often education.[2] A list of such areas was sent first to the British High Commission in Kampala and was later made available to those working in the resettlement offices of the URB centres. Basically and predictably, 'red areas' consisted of the inner London boroughs, the Birmingham conurbation, Leicester, and the textile towns of Yorkshire, all of which had, in addition to the qualifications noted above, large immigrant communities.

Originally, the areas were labelled 'black' and 'white' respectively, but due to possible racial overtones, were later called 'red' and 'green.'

Although intended for uses internal to the URB and the resettlement process, the publishing of lists of red and green areas in the press brought wide-ranging criticism to the Board. It is not entirely clear what priority the Government placed on the actual dispersal of the refugees. To be sure, dispersal was an avowed policy of the Resettlement Board. Critics have suggested that the policy merely was one of political expediency — that it was more important to the Government that the British people believe the Asians were being spread around the country than it was to actually disperse them.

Indeed, the two major components of the Board's relocation strategy did seem incompatible: (1) that the immigrants be encouraged to take the major responsibility for their own resettlement; and (2) that they be discouraged from going into those very areas where the large Asian communities were located, and in which the new arrivals could expect to receive the most assistance. A substantial number of those arriving in September and October went directly from the airports to locations in the United Kingdom and were encouraged to do so. Others were essentially overnight guests at one of the resettlement centres, using the facility as a transit camp. Almost all headed for destinations in the red areas. The effects of the resettlement operations on these refugees were minimal.

Movement through the resettlement centres in the early days of their operation also reflected the basic desire to get the refugees out into the community as quickly as possible. The most efficient way of accomplishing this task was to encourage as much initiative on the part of the refugees themselves as possible. In fact, a large proportion of even those Asians going to resettlement centres in the early days found accommodations and work in Britain with help, not from the resettlement officers, but rather from friends, relatives, or other contacts in the United Kingdom who were not inhibited by 'red area' designations. The resettlement officers generally tried to dissuade families from going into the 'red areas' unless the ties to that area were close ones, but few of the immigrants with a strong desire to go to the urban Asian communities did not do so. At Greenham Common, one of the largest centres throughout its operation, 148 families departed between 7th and 15th October. Of these, 88 went to Greater London and 16 to Leicester.[3] In almost every case, these families were going to accommodations for which they had made their own arrangements.

Local Response

Throughout most of the fall, public opinion remained negative among the large multiracial communities in Greater London and other urban areas. Faced with crowded schools, housing shortages, and over-burdened social services and health agencies, no one expected a welcome mat to be laid out for the refugees. Members of the Uganda Resettlement Board staff toured communities across Britain to emphasise the Board's awareness of local problems and to indicate how the Government hoped to ease any burden. In many of these areas, no council housing was available. Long waiting lists had existed for years. Many of the people on such lists qualified for housing based upon earlier moves necessitated by urban development. A five-year residential qualification existed in most boroughs; a person must have spent four years in the London area and the last year in the borough in which he wanted to establish permanent residence. Council housing was out of the question for new arrivals. One of the highly immigrant-populated boroughs, Ealing, called the Town Council into a special session to discuss the impending crisis. Newspapers reported 'angry scenes outside the town hall' as the meeting progressed. Alderman Robert Hetherington stated at the meeting, 'The message is very clear from the council — we just cannot take any more people, whatever their race, colour, or creed.' The Ealing Council in a rational action decided to write to the Home Office to ask that any resettlement policy adopted for the new arrivals not add to Ealing's 'existing problems.'[4]

A *Times* reporter covering the second official meeting of the Resettlement Board on September 7 said that the meeting 'did little to dispel the uncertainty that surrounds detailed plans for the resettlement and reception of Asians expelled from Uganda.'[5] The following day, the Board, seeking to gain public confidence and to reduce the tension level in communities expecting a large Asian influx, made public important steps to be taken by the Government. Three avenues by which local authorities could secure funds were set forth: (1) through special arrangements under a rate support grant system; (2) through specific grants under Section 11 of the Local Government Act of 1966 to employ extra staff, in schools, for example; and (3) through the Uganda Resettlement Board. The Board was given discretion to make payments toward the costs incurred by local authorities for those items which would not generally be considered an integral part of a community's usual programme expenditure. The Board could pay up to full costs for temporary arrangements made over a period of a year by local units receiving the immigrants.

The strong commitment from the Home Secretary to meet the local costs of resettling Ugandan Asians, and to do so with a minimum of red tape, helped to ease some of the hostility voiced by local communities. Before the announcement of that commitment, only a small number of communities had been willing to take a few families. For example, when Peterborough had offered fifty homes to Ugandan Asians, such a local outcry resulted that the City Council explained its position in a special newspaper which was distributed to 30,000 people. An official commented on the rationale for the newspaper:

> Many of the people who have protested against the Asians coming say we already have enough immigrants living in the city. Others were much more abusive, claiming that immigrants always seemed to get priority over English people. Because of this, we felt the issue ought to be put into its proper perspective.[6]

Most communities were conscious of their responsibility to assist any family taking up residence, no matter what their origin.

The overall problem faced by City Councils, seeking to come to grips with a potential crisis situation, was to answer the question: 'How many?' Perhaps, the Brent 'Civic Review' summarised it best:

> In every possible way, the Council was prepared to meet the situation, but it was short of the one vital piece of information. How many? All the wishful thinking of the Council and residents would do nothing to prevent some Asians coming to Brent; there were no powers that could be used to prevent them so doing but again the question was, 'How many?'
>
> What will happen is difficult to predict, but one thing is certain: Brent has taken all steps which are reasonable and practicable in light of the knowledge which it has, to prepare for a possible influx and, although it reiterates that it does not wish the door to be thrown open in the invitation to those Asians, if they come to Brent, we shall do our best to afford them such reasonable facilities as are compatible with our own needs.[7]

Praful Patel, Resettlement Board member and Secretary of the Committee on United Kingdom Citizenship, commented on the worry going on about 'How many?' He said: 'It is absolutely absurd and stupid for people to guess how many will go to Birmingham, Leicester, Brent, or Basingstoke.' There is no question that the 'numbers game' added to the danger of racial conflict mentioned off and on in British newspapers throughout the fall.

The distribution of relocated Asian refugees for November 1, 1972 shows a high percentage concentrated in a very few regions — the red areas, notably Greater London and, to a distinctly lesser but still important degree, the East Midlands (Table I).[8] Both of these areas had anticipated the influx and especially in the case of Leicester, continuing tactics to discourage immigration were evident. The Government had counted on the ability of most of the Asians to make their own way. Despite some official disappointment at the rate this was occurring, the immigrants were indeed accomplishing the task. Ultimately, over two-thirds of the Asian immigrants did not depend on the Board to assist with their housing or employment, and they went where they chose.

Through the months of November and December, a modification was occurring in the destination patterns of the Asians. The reliance of increasing numbers of the immigrant families on resettlement office assistance began to produce a greater dispersal.

A comparison of the destination figures for January 1, 1973 with those of November 1, 1972, reveal the impact that the resettlement officers were beginning to have (Table I). By November 1, almost 60 per cent of the immigrants had gone to the London boroughs and an additional 15 per cent to the East Midlands, particularly to Leicester. During the following two months, only 2,700 out of the 8,400 leaving the centres went to London, dropping its share of the total of relocated immigrants to 47.6 per cent. This had been accomplished through marked, though not spectacular, increases in all the other regions except the East Midlands.[9]

In addition to the tendency for an increasingly large share of those in the centres to rely on URB assistance in relocating, a second trend began to influence the dispersal patterns. A large proportion of the Asian families relocated by the resettlement offices in the early weeks of the operation was placed in private dwellings. But through the months of November and December, the importance of Council housing began to increase. The distribution of private dwellings offered to the URB for rental to Asians more closely resembled the population distribution in the United Kingdom than did that of the local authority housing.[10] The greater the reliance on local authority housing became, the more the Asians began appearing in areas not on the 'red' list. In January, URB staff members suggested that if all local authority housing listed with the Board would become available, most of the remaining families in the centres could be accommodated.[11] Unfortunately , such was not to be the case, and the impact of the Board on dispersal patterns would not be as profound as had been hoped.

Accommodating the Asians

If indeed the real problem associated with relocating the Asians was the dearth of housing in Britain, how had the Board attempted to find accommodation for those refugees who could not locate it for themselves? When the dimensions of the Asian influx were determined, the British public was asked to respond to the imminent housing crisis, and many did. By September, 2,000 places in private homes had been offered. Political and religious leaders offered accommodations to refugee families. *Punch* suggested that indeed it was *de rigueur* to have an

Table I

INITIAL DESTINATIONS OF UGANDAN ASIANS

Region	As of November 1		As of January 1	
	Number	% of Total	Number	% of Total
North	41	·38%	231	1·19%
Northwest	430	3·95%	1179	6·19%
West Midlands	745	6·93%	1751	9·06%
East Anglia	157	1·44%	341	1·76%
Yorkshire-Humberside	234	2·15%	645	3·34%
Southeast	801	7·36%	1852	9·58%
Scotland	42	0·39%	386	2·00%
Wales	99	0·91%	321	1·66%
Southwest	162	1·49%	669	3·46%
East Midlands	1653	15·19%	2747	14·22%
London	6464	59·40%	9197	47·58%
TOTALS	10,883		19,322	

Source: URB data

Asian in the neighbourhood.[12] While the motives behind some offers were questionable, the major outpouring was clearly a humanitarian response by the British public. Eventually, some 5,000 offers of private housing for the Asians were made.[13] Each potential residence was visited by a member of the Women's Royal Voluntary Service (1) to guarantee that the offer was a genuine one and (2) to check on the size, condition of the residence and terms of occupancy. A county-by-county listing was then assembled by the Board.

A great deal of publicity and some good will was generated in the process. Unfortunately, the Board found most of the housing unusable. Some properties offered were not in sufficiently good condition to merit approval. A more frequent problem, however, was the shortness of the term of availability or the time the property was available. Local authorities agreed to overlook temporary violation of the regulations on the numbers of people living in private housing. Shortages of space, cookers, sinks, water closets, and baths all were disregarded in order to allow the accommodation of relatives or friends from among the refugees.

Although about 1,500 of the offers were forwarded to the centres, private housing did little to alleviate the problems besetting the resettlement officers. Most families were better served by being housed in the centres and staying there until proper quarters were found. One senior resettlement officer put it succinctly, 'Placing families in temporary housing is only storing up our troubles for later.'14

The call then went out to the public sector. Each local authority was asked for any of its own housing which could be made available and any blocks of housing available in their area. The response was mixed. Some authorities did not have housing to offer. Others had such great pressure on those accommodations that were, or would be, available, that they considered it inappropriate or impolitic to give these to the Board.

Not all the responses were negative. Certain parts of the United Kingdom, particularly those areas of high unemployment, had a surplus of Council housing. Other local authorities, despite being hard pressed and having long waiting lists, offered housing under the condition that the fact would not be made known publicly. Still others, flying in the face of certain criticism, made their decision based on what some described as socially responsible reasons.

One rich source of public housing were the homes owned by the Commission for the New Towns. Of those 30,000 dwellings, about 80 became vacant each month. This rate of turnover caused some authorities to suggest that provisions of these to Asians would cause only a few months' delay for people waiting for New Town homes.

By January 1, almost 2,100 local authority houses in over 340 local authority areas had been offered to the URB.15 This number could have gone a long way toward solving the housing problem. Unfortunately, the impact was reduced significantly for a number of reasons. The availability of the dwellings was in many cases not immediate. Many were relets and would become available over a period of weeks or months. Others were being completed and were not yet ready for occupancy at the time they were offered to the URB. Still others were tied to employment – a job in the area had to be obtained before the Council would agree to accept a refugee family.16

A second cause of problems was the location of the Council accommodations. Most were in parts of the United Kingdom either undesirable or unknown to the refugees. By the same token, few offers had come from local authorities in areas that the Asians felt were highly desirable. In Table II, the uneven geographic distribution of Council housing offers in the United Kingdom can be seen. London and the East Midlands show the most noticeable dearth of offers, but this was a predictable response from these desirable and hard-pressed areas. Scotland, on the other hand, produced over 300 local authority accommodations, but this was a region which the Asians viewed with some reluctance. It was expected that the distribution of available

Table II

LOCAL AUTHORITY HOUSING OFFERS

Region	Offered as of January 1, 1973[1]	Occupied[2]
Northern	220	65
Yorkshire	218	132
East Midlands	171	91
Scotland	301	150
Wales	95	61
Southwest	214	139
Southeast	357	233
East Anglia		59
West Midlands	196	124
Northwest	249	159
London	75	58
	2,096	1,271

[1] URB data obtained in personal interviews, January 1973.

[2] As of URB interim report, April 1973.

Council housing could assist the Resettlement Board in dispersing the Asians in the United Kingdom. Whether it would work out that way was yet to be discerned.

How did the Board handle the housing that it did have available? Accommodations in a particular region were allotted in the main to resettlement centres located in that region. This was meant to provide the resettlement officers with a better opportunity to 'sell' their houses to the Asian families. It was possible to arrange for some families to visit a potential place of relocation before deciding whether to accept the offer.

Many of the Council houses assigned to a centre were not located in the centre's locale. This was particularly true of centres in relatively isolated locations; for example, that at Doniford in the west country of England. Doniford Centre's listing of accommodations was from its own region, but those amounted to just over one quarter of the accommodations it was attempting to distribute to the Asian families. Almost as many assigned to the Centre were from Scotland.

Maresfield Resettlement Centre had an even more difficult problem on its hands. As of January 1, of the 60 Council houses remaining on its listing, 49 of them were in Scotland. Despite the 'tremendous cooperation' of the authorities in Scotland and the 'eagerness' which they displayed with respect to housing the Asians, selling the idea of going to a place so unfamiliar to the refugees was not any easier at Maresfield than it was at other centres.[17]

The Asians coming from Uganda had a strong orientation toward urban areas. They knew of London and Leicester and only a few of the other major cities in England. It was difficult for them to understand that many more urban centres in the United Kingdom could offer the amenities and, more importantly, the economic opportunities they sought.

It was not only a reluctance to go to Scotland which complicated matters. Scotland, of course, seemed like the Arctic Circle to many of the Asians. Council housing in other areas as well was being turned down by families. Some had a clear notion of where they would like to go and were unwilling to settle for other locations. Often these preferences were based on the location of friends or relatives in Britain and thus, typically, were for those areas where the URB had no housing available.

Even at Maresfield, which had been criticised for its facilities and its morale, a number of families turned down local authority housing to stay at the Centre. They were, it appeared, more willing to accept known discomforts than unknown possibilities, at least during the early weeks in the United Kingdom.

Many families, of course, were accepting offers of housing and leaving the centres. With their departure, the Resettlement Board's responsibilities for the families ceased. Disquieting information, however, was reaching the Board about conditions the Asians were encountering.

A survey conducted by the International Voluntary Service in four London boroughs found that 76 per cent of the families were in temporary accommodations, and that almost half were either seriously overcrowded or faced eviction.[18] Of the 1,000 Ugandan Asians in the four boroughs, 57 per cent had been processed through resettlement centres and were considered by the Board to be 'resettled.' The report recommended that the Board accept a continuing responsibility for the Asians. In a predictable response, the Board claimed it had no facilities for caring for the refugees after they had left airports or centres.

Almost all of those who had found their way to the four London boroughs included in the survey, had done so on their own. Even those who had made use of a resettlement centre had arranged their own accommodation and had had little, if anything, to do with the resettlement officers.

As of January 1, the resettlement centres had a population of 7,775 out of the 21,281 which had entered them during a six-week period beginning in late September. Fourteen of the original sixteen centres

82

were still open, but three closed within days. The relocation operation continued to proceed without major incident so that at the time of the Board's interim report in April, the population had fallen to 3,380 at three centres,[19] and by July it was down to 2,000. The rate of departures progressively slowed in the months that followed so that the last centre did not close its doors until January 1974.

The work of the centres and the work of the Board were in the final stages. But the story of the immigrants clearly was not. While the Asians had been 'relocated,' critics claim that few had been 'resettled.' The 'real story' may *not* be about the 20 per cent in council housing upon whom the Board's operations had the most major impact and who may indeed have been resettled.[20] The real story may have been of those who selected the areas 'coloured' by the URB in brightest red, and for whom major problems still needed solutions. As traumatic as were the events in Uganda, as unfamiliar as were the environments of resettlement centres, the real test of the resiliency and adaptability of the refugee families was just beginning.

Notes

1. For example, the *Uganda Argus.*
2. Personal interviews – Mr T.A. Critchley, London, January 1973 and Sir Charles Cunningham, London, January 30, 1973.
3. Computed from Greenham Common Resettlement Office data, January 1973.
4. Quoted in The *Guardian*, September 21, 1972.
5. The *Times*, September 8, 1972.
6. The *Times*, September 7, 1972.
7. *Brent Civic Review*, October 1972, p. 2.
8. Data from Uganda Resettlement Board weekly status reports. The URB was hesitant about revealing publicly the destinations of the Asians because (1) the Board felt the figures could raise anxieties in the local communities, thus making resettlement more difficult, and (2) the Board was convinced that the initial destinations stated by many of the Asians would often be only temporary places of residence. A good deal of evidence, including that from a survey in London's Wandsworth borough which is detailed later in this study, tends to confirm the Board's assumption of a high degree of mobility among the refugees in the first months after their arrival.
9. Scotland shows the sharpest jump, a fivefold increase, clearly the result of placing of Asian families in Council housing.
10. Three and one-half times as many people were placed by the resettlement officers in private dwellings in London as in Council housing.
11. Personal interviews, URB Headquarters, London, January 4, 1973.
12. *Punch*, October 25, 1972, pp. 579-81.
13. Information from URB data obtained in personal interviews, January 4, 1973.
14. Personal interview.
15. URB data, January 1973.
16. At Tonfanau Resettlement Centre, 49 out of the 144 Council houses on their listings as of January 1, 1973 were job linked. Four had just been

returned to URB Headquarters due to the impossibility of filling the job requirements from among the centre residents. Information obtained from Resettlement Office data, Tonfanau, Wales, January 8-9, 1973.

17. W. Fisher, Senior Resettlement Officer, Maresfield, personal interview, December 28, 1972.
18. 'International Voluntary Service Survey of Camden, Brent, Ealing and Wandsworth Boroughs,' (London, December, 1972).
19. URB Interim Report, HMSO, April 1973.
20. D. Humphry and M. Ward, *Sunday Times*, June 10, 1973.

6. WANDSWORTH: A HOST COMMUNITY

As it became evident that almost all of the Asians would be going to the major urban centres in the United Kingdom — especially London — Wandsworth, a multiracial inner London borough south of the Thames, began preparing to accept a sudden influx of people. This host community initiated steps to help the arrivals make the transitional adjustment to British society.

Immigrants are not a new phenomenon in Wandsworth. One out of every ten people in the borough comes either from Asia or from the West Indies. Wandsworth claims slightly more than 300,000 inhabitants and contains one of the largest Asian populations in Britain, including a heavy concentration of East African Asians. Other London boroughs have experienced similar, and in some cases, a greater influx of immigrants. The point is simply that at both the national and the local level, a pattern of response has evolved to create a 'mobilisation of bias' when the political system acts to change its policies with respect to newcomers. This bias is naturally extended or already dominant in national patterns, and it is visible in the Greater London area. The argument is not whether the Wandsworth borough response is typical. In fact, it may have been atypical, i.e. there may have been a more consciously organised response to ease acceptance than in some other areas. Nevertheless, the context in which the community responded seemed quite typical of those considerations necessary in most London boroughs as well as in fairly large communities throughout Great Britain, to begin the process of acculturation. Of course, the analysis in this chapter should not be considered more than documentation of one case in which a particular community helped a group of Ugandan Asians (1) to begin the process of resettlement and (2) begin the development of an expanding social field in a new community.

Wandsworth attracted Ugandan Asian migrants when many other communities in Great Britain did not. One could offer several explanations for this. Chief among the virtues that the group of new residents saw was the existence of an Asian community. Predictably, most people attempted to relocate with or near families and friends, or at least in neighbourhoods characterised by lifeways familiar and comfortable to the Asians. Naturally, areas with large Asian populations and, more specifically, with East African Asian populations tended, in spite of concerted government efforts to disperse the refugees, to inherit a larger proportion of the inflow than did communities with

85

small or no Indian cultural groups. This clustering tendency is one which promotes segregation: recognition of this fact led to Wandsworth's being labelled by the Uganda Resettlement Board as a 'red area.'

Official projections of the number of Ugandan Asians who would come to Wandsworth were high. On the basis of a survey conducted in Kampala the URB projected that 600 would settle in the borough. Migrants who did settle in Wandsworth did so, no doubt, in large part because others of comparable background had managed to carve out a cultural and social niche there. This offered the newcomers some reprieve from the relatively foreign ways of the British. Since Wandsworth is by no means homogeneous, or largely Asian, or even largely minority in population, the community is racially and socially mixed; neighbourhoods, though, retain a fairly distinct racial, ethnic and class composition. Among alternatives open to the Ugandan Asians, communities such as Wandsworth provided natural havens in a time of separation from a familiar and once secure way of life. The opportunity to re-establish the social field in such a natural haven was perhaps easier than in other dominantly white British communities. Of course, the main obstacles to permanent settlement were housing and employment conditions.

Employment and Housing Conditions

What sort of employment climate existed in the borough in the early spring of 1973? Responding in part to the Greater London Council's plan for population and economic realignment, the employment situation in the region had been going through considerable change over the past several years. Manufacturing had declined notably. Rather than seeking out new industrial concerns, developers were more likely to construct an office building. Such shifts in employment patterns were beginning to affect the population makeup of the borough. An older, skilled population with strong roots in the community were beginning to find themselves out of work. If office complexes were to become the major employment enterprises, then women would be needed to serve as the major work force. Women living in the area, however, were not trained for this type of work. Many of the male work force were forced to move on with manufacturing plants. This is one of several reasons why many of the inner London boroughs have been losing population over the past several years. The ten-year change in population for Wandsworth shows a 10 per cent decrease. Although the Wandsworth borough boundaries had changed during this period, the *1971 Annual Abstract of Greater London Statistics* uses approximate figures for 1961 to show a downward trend from 335,000 in 1961, to

301,000 in 1971.[1] The inner London boroughs as a group decreased 14 per cent, or 447,000 during the same period.

The housing outlook also appeared bleak at the close of 1972. As of December 31, 1972, there were 22,671 Wandsworth Borough Council-owned dwellings and 10,418 Greater London Council-owned dwellings in Wandsworth.[2] Estimates are that 800 to 900 dwellings will be added during each of the next several years. These additional units, as well as turnover in the present dwellings, are insufficient to meet current needs. That December, 7,000 families were on the waiting list — 2,000 were eligible and in need. Another 3,000 on the list would be eligible when they met the residence requirement, but they too were in need. Another 2,000 on the list, however, were not considered in particularly great need. The dependence on government-built and managed housing for much of the low income population in inner London was supported by the National Government and the Greater London Council. However, prospects for relief were dim in the near future, and they certainly would be of no help to the Ugandan Asians over the next five years, i.e. the years necessary in any event to meet the residency requirement. One local leader observed: 'It would take a serious commitment from the National Government to solve the housing problem.' He added, 'We want the Greater London Council and the Government to build more homes in outer London . . . . We do not want money as much as we would like to see housing built outside of the area.'

Some local authorities have provided up to 100 per cent loans with few strings attached. As one scholar has observed: 'Local authorities have regarded the granting of mortgages as a social service, and many take the view that it is a useful way of preventing deterioration of older houses. With the emphasis on older, cheaper houses, many of these schemes have been of immense help to immigrants.'[3] In Wandsworth, a 100 per cent borough loan was rare, and a loan for a house worth more than £9,500 was against recommended guidelines. The problem was that almost no housing was available at that low a price. Many Asian leaders and community officials were of the opinion that the loans ought to be extended to £12,000, that is, to housing prices necessary to make a purchase. There was no great rush by the officials to extend owner occupation. Also, any improvement in borough policies would make the borough more attractive to non-residents. There was no desire to make Wandsworth stand apart from any other of the thirty-two London boroughs. Under these conditions, people were forced to rent what was available, and such accommodations generally turned out to be priced unreasonably high and/or were in poor condition.

The Putney Group[4]

To take a cold, hard look at the problem of absorbing 'new immigrants,' a group of community elders got together one early September evening in the town of Putney. This 'Putney group' was composed of a highly responsible 'elite' representing various interests in the community. Rumours, 'red areas,' racial climate, housing shortages, large numbers, etc. were problems mentioned as to why something had to be done. As community leaders, they agreed to reach an understanding informally and quietly on how Wandsworth best could meet the needs of the refugees and still maintain a calm, sensible climate of opinion among the native British, West Indians, Indians, Pakistanis, and settled East African Asians.

Estimates of immigrant numbers varied considerably. Some rumours indicated potential thousands. Designation of Wandsworth as a 'red area' served to increase the rumours and to heighten the concern. One widely circulated rumour gave figures on the numbers of blind and diseased who were coming to Wandsworth. All kinds of stories were mentioned. Most, including those about large numbers of diseased or blind Asians were totally unfounded. Although racial overtones in the community were noted, for the most part these seemed subdued and possible to control through a thoughtful low-key reaction to the crisis.

The elders were disturbed with the general concept of 'red areas' and were irritated that the designation of the borough as a 'red area' was done without consulting them. They believed that the red area designation would be ineffectual in reducing the number of refugees who would come to the borough. Restrictions were not rigid for those who lived with relatives or good friends in a London borough, and furthermore the 'red area' designation did not apply to those who could pay their own air fares from Uganda. They were as free as British citizens to come and go, and to settle anywhere. Moreover, the 'red area' tag focused attention on the Asians, aroused concern among the natives, and frustrated the new immigrants as well as old. Under these conditions, prospects for acceptance were difficult.

Considerable agreement was found among the 'Putney group' in terms of similarities between this sudden influx and the Kenyan Asian arrivals in 1968. Details were given regarding how a network between Wandsworth and Kenya had operated to bring families to the borough in 1968. Many believed that this experience had shown the need for under-reaction rather than for over-reaction. For instance, educators recalled that many thought the school enrolments were going to swell to the point of requiring construction of new facilities in 1968. The Kenyan Asians did join their friends and relatives in Wandsworth. In the natural process of finding housing and employment, though, families scattered inside and outside the borough. Thus no single area had to accommodate large numbers of children and no new facilities were needed. Educational leaders were of the opinion that the new influx would work in much the same way. (In January 1973, educators were doing nothing more than attempting to keep an accurate count on new admissions and taking a wait-and-see attitude.)

The presence of these Kenyan Asians and Ugandan Asians who came before Amin's decree meant in all probability that a sizable number would come to the borough — red area or not. The original URB estimate of 600 proved to be reasonably accurate. The 'Putney group' felt that these people would come to settle with friends and relatives. It was anticipated that most of these new arrivals would be of the same socioeconomic levels as those already living in the borough. Opinion held that the new arrivals would probably have a similar outlook on life and prove to be as industrious. They would not want to be dependent on welfare services. They would be willing to help themselves in getting ahead. Therefore, all concerned agreed that the best strategy for dealing with the impending crisis was to help the Asians help themselves. The consensus was that all problems associated with the Ugandan Asian influx would be handled by the Community Relations Officer, Charles Boxer, and his staff. The 'Putney group' would work informally with the CRO, but Boxer's responsibility would be to sort the real from the imaginary problems. The basic attitude expressed at that meeting, and reiterated throughout the transitional phase of settlement, was that the burden of handling the crisis should be placed directly on the CRO's shoulders. Overall, the strategy conceived at the Putney meeting determined the direction of the community's response for the initial six-month transitional phase of the crisis.

Views of Borough Councillors

The Wandsworth Borough Council was aware of the direction and intensity, i.e. the low-key approach of the response to the Asian situation. In an interview with the Council leader, Ian McGarry, he emphasised that the Council would look to the Community Relations Officer for direction in responding to the needs of the new immigrants.[5] He said that the Council recognised their need to take some direct responsibility at a proper point in time. After the transitional phase had been weathered, the real dimensions of the problem would be obvious. At that time, Mr McGarry was confident that the Council would make some policy decisions to deal specifically with the Ugandan Asians.

A less optimistic point of view was taken by a Conservative spokesman on the Wandsworth Council, D.T.L. Mallam. After a September meeting of the heads of the Asian communities in Wandsworth and representatives of the Council and the Community Relations Office, he said, 'We must do our utmost to discourage them from coming to Wandsworth.' He observed that many would come due to the presence of others of their own race and due to the work opportunities in the London area. He noted Wandsworth's problems in housing and education:

> We have a large housing waiting list and, even though a considerable majority on that list have little or no need, we have at the top of the list many with a great need; we also have something in excess of 100 families who are homeless and some of these are having to put up with bed and breakfast accommodations.[6]

Several other councillors expressed concern with the notion of how helpful or responsive they should be in comparison with the seemingly tough point of view being taken by other London boroughs. The councillors were of the opinion that if Wandsworth took a 'soft approach,' i.e. developed more lenient policies, many Ugandan Asians from across London would move to Wandsworth. Careful attention was given to the policies and expressed opinions of other boroughs. Yet, the councillors felt that the Wandsworth Council had to be realistic enough to be prepared to help those in real need, if and when their present situation became such that all opportunities for alternative solutions disappeared.

Several councillors reported in interviews that to help the Council do the right things, i.e. to do what they must in face of constituent counter-pressures, the CRO, Charles Boxer, would have to produce a 'controlled demonstration of need.' This seemed to translate into enough noise to be heard but not enough to be inflammable or uncontrollable. The reluctance to act without considerable available evidence was voiced by one councillor who recognised the counter-reaction of constituents:

> I have had a considerable number of disturbing letters from people saying we were born and bred in this borough. We have lived here for 30 years. We have been on the waiting list for 15 years and here come these Asians into the borough and they get houses. Of course, the Asians have not got any housing. [7]

The councillor went on to point out that the Ugandan Asians were not eligible due to failure to meet residence requirements.

The Community Relations Approach

The dominant community relations approach in Great Britain calls for

90

the bringing together of two communities, the 'hosts' and the 'immigrants.' Each should recognise that they have common interests. They should join in a cooperative effort to create a unified common community.[8] Such a host/immigrant framework is criticised on the grounds that it implies that the immigrant must be the one to change his pattern of behaviour, to conform to the dominant culture of the host society.[9] The concept of different groups working toward common ends has been labelled a 'cooperative rationality.' Where people work toward consensus and avoid conflict: '. . . the set goals must favour no special interests, must be noncontroversial, and must be in the community's best interest; that is, they must contribute to increasing community solidarity and to reducing community conflict and strain.'[10]

The Community Relations Officer for the Wandsworth borough, Charles Boxer, put it this way: 'I work in a borough of a third of a million people. It is a very mixed borough. It has old housing, new housing; rich and poor live together over a fairly large area. Our responsibility is to help the immigrants settle down, to get the host community to accept immigrants, and to help the immigrants with particular problems that they have.'[11]

Charles Boxer works for the Wandsworth Council for Community Relations (WCCR). It was formed in 1967 and is 'committed to the idea of seeing harmonious relationships established and maintained between the "old" and the "new" residents of the borough.'[12] It is one of many Community Relations Councils across Great Britain taking its lead from the Community Relations Commission (CRC). This national body coordinates and guides the work of the local Community Relations Councils. It has two major goals: to ensure the civil rights of immigrants, and to lessen prejudice and encourage racial harmony. Locally, the WCCR stresses that it is an 'independent and autonomous body and not an off-shoot of the Town Hall.'[13] The WCCR emphasises that it receives important support from the Borough Council, CRC, the Inner London Education Authority, and the Department of Employment. Policy for the WCCR is determined by a volunteer Executive Committee composed of a wide cross-section of the local community, including Borough Council, immigrant and other community groups, and education, youth and welfare services. The WCCR, as can be seen by their own words below, follows the general host/immigrant theme laid down for Community Relations Councils across Great Britain:

Some hardship and misunderstanding is inevitable in almost any community. Where the mix of the neighbourhood had roots deep in the past, hardships are often sympathetically shared and misunderstandings quietly resolved.

Where a community is a mix of 'old' and 'new' residents or, more particularly, 'host' and former 'immigrant,' misunderstandings are sometimes magnified. Hardships are less easily borne.

The new Wandsworth, with its invaluable mix of types, classes, beliefs, races and cultures, is such a community. The aim of the WCCR is to see that all of us in Wandsworth recognise the positive contribution we can make to the lives of each other, and the ease with which problems can be discussed and shared. It is the task of the WCCR to improve not just the climate of understanding but the lot of anyone who, in his search for work, a home, better education or simple everyday living, has fallen foul of individuals, authority or the community at large because of ignorance or discrimination.

From its beginning, the WCCR has tried to serve the community in two important ways — as an initiator of new ideas and schemes for the development of good relations between all communities within the borough, and as a haven to which minority groups and others can turn when people and events militate against them.[14]

In this process, the relationship of the WCCR to local authorities is crucial. The recent study by Hill and Issacharoff points out that Community Relations Councils in general are not in an easy situation, even though they are voluntary organisations. They cannot use all the pressure group strategies to gain public attention because they are quasi-statutory bodies dependent on the support of a Government-managed national agency. These groups have no statutory powers of their own and cannot force local authorities to cooperate or even, in some cases, acknowledge their existence. The authors note: 'The structure which the CRC prescribes for local communities implies what we shall call an "*elite strategy*", community involvement through securing the support of all the most powerful elements in the community.'[15]

The Operation of the WCCR

In an interview, Charles Boxer[16] reported two major problems to be dealt with in the emerging crisis: (1) creating sufficient political support to get the community to take some supportive steps, and (2) providing welfare and information to the refugees who arrived in Wandsworth. Boxer noted: 'First, we felt that the Asian groups could give us a lot of support in getting information to the new arrivals and in offering to provide houses. We knew that the Asian groups would be the ones who would suffer anyway, unless we built them up and gave them some kind of support and strength.' Boxer related that meetings were called with Asian leaders during the first weeks of September as the estimates of 600 arrivals became known and as refugees started to arrive by plane loads. He praised the strong support efforts of the Asian groups. The CRO brought the Asian groups and Town Hall representatives together during the beginning weeks of the crisis and again during the winter, as needs for housing became increasingly clear. Boxer said: 'These meetings gave the Asian community representatives an opportunity to express their opinion at a high point in official discussions, and also to act as a pressure group on the politician to make him move.' At the same time, Boxer said, attempts were made to achieve the real political solution, i.e. to support the concept of having private housing associations with Borough Council financing help the new arrivals secure accommodations.

The WCCR organised its response to the Ugandan Asian refugee situation as a short-term problem in the borough. According to Boxer, the basic idea was to establish contact with all the new families, give available assistance, and identify the major problems. The immediate goals were to provide welfare, information and housing assistance. Cooperating with the Social Services Department and the Borough Council, a full-time welfare worker and a secretary were added to deal directly with the Ugandan Asian families. Monies would be provided by the Uganda Resettlement Board. Employing, on a temporary basis, an East African Asian as the Community Resettlement Officer was the only formal bureaucratic personnel action taken at the borough level.

It was unlikely that agencies would have to make much of an adjustment over the long run. It is not unusual for people unfamiliar with local community agencies to expect that the CRO would be the proper person to provide necessary assistance not only during the transitional phase, but whenever help is needed. One recent book on this subject notes: 'People are going to give their support to an organisation that can do something for them. They are going to expect a concrete response to their own pressing problems. . . .'[17] The authors suggested that social work may be quite necessary to aid the CRO's in establishing rapport, to contact people, to meet new arrivals, and to find out the needs of these people.[18]

Mrs Urmila Patel was appointed Community Resettlement Officer. She was a member of the Gujerat Samaj and had been in Great Britain seven years. She spoke Gujerati and some Hindi and Urdu. Her first task, and not an easy one, was to visit all of the new arrivals. Volunteers helped to locate new arrivals. Lists containing the anticipated addresses of the arrivals were supplied by the Uganda Resettlement Board. At the airport the Asians had filled out forms indicating where they were going. Resettlement centre personnel provided officials in Wandsworth with similar information. Health services and social service agencies also made referrals, but it was impossible to reach people quickly — those supposedly there and those really there — and offer the assistance that was available to help newcomers. To overcome this problem, an Advice Centre was set up in Wandsworth at Upper Tooting Methodist Church where Ugandan Asians could come every Thursday afternoon to receive assistance from voluntary and professional workers.

The Advice Centre
To capture the human drama of resettlement in a large borough was difficult due to the fact that the process was generally carried out in a home on a one-to-one personal basis between a WCCR volunteer (or staffer) and a refugee. Yet, opportunities, such as those provided at the weekly Advice Centre, should be portrayed. Weekly visits to the Wandsworth Community Relations Advice Centre in January 1973 found Mrs Patel and her secretary-administrator, Miss Sandra Bean, creating an environment to welcome immigrants and, more importantly, to show that someone was interested in individual problems. Using the large church hall as a centre of activity, tables and chairs were arranged around the room in small sets. Some people just dropped in to see what was going on, to meet and chat with a friend over a cup of tea, to see what clothing might be available, or perhaps to receive some advice.

Before the Centre opened at 1.30, there would be eight or nine people waiting outside the church. In the first several weeks, over sixty people would 'just drop in' and perhaps get some help. By mid-January, the number would drop to forty-five, and less into February as people found answers to their questions. Some began to find new friends in their neighbourhoods. Each Thursday, six or seven volunteers would each handle an information table. Each had notes pinned to their chest indicating their identity and their area of concern. Assigned tables were provided for such topics as statelessness, education, welfare, housing, language, employment and social security. A relaxed atmosphere prevailed. Several women served tea and cookies. Small groups huddled around each table talking quietly; their children ran around laughing gaily. Men stood in the corner discussing job prospects, and teenagers could be overheard discussing dating problems in Britain and the resultant Asian family reactions.

Generally, only the family being helped would be at the volunteer's table. When one family left the table, another from some corner in the church hall would just 'happen' to stop by the table. Some with a minor problem needed only reassurance that everything would be worked out. Others wanted to find out whether a rumour they heard was true. Some had serious passport problems and were hesitant to talk with immigration officials. They preferred that the volunteers make discreet inquiries.

In most cases, the major problem centred upon crowded housing situations. The common complaint was that several people were crowded into each room of a house designed to be a single family dwelling. Women who needed employment to help their family raise mortgage money were congregated around the language centre table. Many did not have enough English to land any job. Some could not read an underground station map.

Problems among the elderly who could not work and who could not speak the language were apparent among the Advice Centre's visitors. These people seemed to be in the most unfortunate circumstances. They looked lost and dejected. Those with husbands classified as stateless, i.e. either in a stateless camp in Austria or in Malta, wondered aloud about what would happen to them. All they could do was sit and wait. All in all, Thursday afternoon information sessions during the transitional resettlement phase of the crisis were useful. They were an excellent way to reach people and to encourage people to come forward with their problems. The sessions aided in spreading the word about the helpful role of the WCCR, and they helped the WCCR in making an assessment of the seriousness of the situation in order to get the response necessary from the broader community and the Borough Council in particular.

Most of the Asians who came to the Centre praised its service. The only serious criticism came from those Ugandan Asians who saw the Centre's responsibilities as something other than an information centre and 'general help' arm of the WCCR. Some felt that the Community Resettlement Officer should be a chief advocate, a rabble-rouser, if necessary, and a strong Ugandan Asian voice for the WCCR at the Town Hall and in communicating with the National Government. The Resettlement Office, some felt, should correct all group and individual ills uncovered at the Advice Centre. People looking for such a spokesman did not find the Wandsworth response, or that of Mrs Patel for that matter, a satisfactory one. It was not possible to solve a national housing shortage problem by listening to reports of cramped, unpleasant quarters with two or more families living together. In finding solutions to individual family problems and in bringing comfort to the new arrivals, Mrs Patel, her staff and the volunteers did a commendable job. Quietly, unobtrusively, day after day on a one-to-one caseworker basis, solutions were found to the individual problems presented.

First Steps to Permanent Settlement

The progress made during the six-month transitional phase of acceptance rested on deliberate and humane involvement of the CRO and of his community resettlement team, paid and volunteer, in providing information, comfort and direction. However, lack of substantive assistance in providing adequate housing forced over half of the newcomers to live under crowded conditions. Several borough officials felt that steps to provide the necessary housing should be taken. Others thought that officials should drag their feet to encourage people to try 'self-help,' to find their housing without putting an 'unfair burden' on the community. In other words, a whole-hearted acceptance by the community of its responsibility could mean that people who were in fact capable of helping themselves might not. Of course, the lack of housing would discourage people from staying in the borough, and no one was opposed to people moving out of the crowded district. In addition, if the borough took a supportive housing stand, many Ugandan Asians not faring well in other boroughs might be only too willing to be recipients of such hospitality in Wandsworth.

The CRO and Asian groups convened in January 1973 to evolve a strategy for improving the housing situation. Some pressure was applied by the Asians. Councillors, community officials and Asian leaders by mid-February were seriously examining the utility of using the Solon Housing Association. The Borough Council could provide loans to the association to build or convert homes for Ugandan Asians. Under the housing association concept, the Borough Council would provide the money to improve the dwellings and thereafter, a share of the rent would go to the Council. To sanction involvement of the Solon Housing Association as a nonprofit organisation to provide housing for the Ugandan Asians, was to revert to a discarded Council policy. The preference of the majority on the Council was to have the Council itself take responsibility for improving dwellings and thereby to receive all rent income.[19] The first step in changing to the 'Solon policy' was to have Asian leaders meet with the Housing Committee of the Council.

By the end of mid-February, the groups agreed to make the exception and to assist the housing association in meeting the needs of the new arrivals. As Mrs Margaret Morgan, Chairman of the Council's Housing Committee, reported in an interview:

We have in fact agreed to assist the housing association in the borough. The present policy of the borough council is not to give assistance to housing associations because we feel that the borough ought to be providing the housing. But under these special circumstances, we have made an arrangement with the housing association to give them financial assistance to house the Ugandan Asians. We are hoping to deal with this problem soon, because this is the permanent solution.[20]

Several key officials in the community commented on one underlying reason why, after a six-month transitional phase, the Council would now agree to support the housing association. The housing would

96

be provided for what was now perceived to be an industrious, educated, well-mannered group who were more likely than others to pay their rent. These people could be counted on to keep the place in good repair. Also, they were the type that made good use of public supported housing to serve an immediate need, but who were likely to move to better housing and jobs as opportunities presented themselves. Observers of this type of phenomenon in Great Britain argue that: 'The biggest bias of all is the basic philosophy of public housing in Britain — "informed," in the words of an American critic, "by the Victorian connection that cleanliness and sanitation will in themselves produce satisfaction, if not saintliness." ' As explained by author Elizabeth Burney:

> The principle is simple: A clean person gets a clean house and a dirty person gets a dirty house. Quiet, clean steady-earning families with not more than three children are highly prized because they make life easy for management and their neighbours.[21]

In conclusion, the important point is that the process went according to the Putney group strategy. The low-key approach brought little inflammatory local reaction, and racial overtones remained subdued. The use of traditional committees of the Council and the use of the Community Relations Office to supplement regular community services had worked to keep the situation relatively quiet. The lack of public interest in general, and the lack of 'public' discussion by community officials, allowed the Community Resettlement Officer, Department of Employment, etc. to work on a one-to-one basis to ease the transition of the new arrivals.

More importantly, Asians had helped Asians withstand the early period of adjustment whether the residents had been relatives, friends or members of Asian community groups. Their impact is difficult to measure. There was no question that the self-help of Asians among Asians was substantial. As the magnitude (or perhaps more appropriately, the lack of magnitude) of the refugee influx became understood, the Council finally began to take at least minimum positive steps in easing the adjustment while remaining determined to provide no more assistance than any other London borough. Community leaders were satisfied with the way the informal system had responded. They believed that probably a year or two would be needed to solve some of the problems associated with the influx. Some Asians would never find jobs. Many would remain in inadequate housing. But as a 'red area' Wandsworth had not been totally overburdened with new-comers. The Asians had helped themselves where the community failed to offer direction. For those who were able to help themselves, both they and the community were well served. Nevertheless, for those who suffered through the forced migration and found a hesitant community afraid to do too much too soon, the experience was painful.

Notes

1. 1971 *Annual Abstract of Greater London Statistics*, Greater London Council, Vol. 6, 1972, Table 2.03, p. 20.
2. *Op. cit.*, Table 8.05 and 8.06, pp. 226-227.
3. Elizabeth Burney, *Housing on Trial: A Study of Immigrants and Local Government* (London: Oxford University Press, 1967), p. 51.
4. This section has been pieced together from interviews with formal and informal Wandsworth leaders who attended the meeting.
5. Interviewed, January 1973.
6. *The South London News*, September 18, 1972.
7. Interview, January 1973.
8. Michael J. Hill and Ruth M. Issacharoff, *Community Action and Race Relations* (London: Oxford University Press, 1971), p. 166.
9. J. Rex and R. Moore, *Race, Community and Conflict* (London: Oxford University Press, 1967), p. 13-14.
10. R. Morris and M. Rein, *Social Work Practice* (New York: Columbia University Press, 1962), p. 127.
11. Interviewed, January 1973.
12. Wandsworth Council for Community Relations Informational Brochure, p. 2.
13. *Ibid., loc. cit.*
14. *Ibid., loc. cit.*
15. Hill and Issacharoff, *op. cit.*, p. 60.
16. Interviewed, January 1973.
17. Hill and Issacharoff, *op. cit.*, p. 174.
18. *Ibid., loc. cit.*
19. Information provided by Mrs Margaret Morgan, Chairman, Housing Committee for the Wandsworth Borough Council, January 1973.
20. *Ibid.*
21. Burney, *loc. cit.*

7.   UGANDAN ASIANS IN TWO COMMUNITIES: A SOCIAL PROFILE

What can be predicted from this early stage of settlement about the Asians' future and prospects for absorption in Great Britain? Had they in fact adopted a stance accepting their new home, and did their social and cultural characteristics prepare them for reasonably rapid acculturation? In attempting to answer these questions and to predict the success of the population's adjustment, interviews designed to tap responses and traits of the recently arrived migrants were conducted with all Ugandan Asian heads-of-households[1] settling in two selected communities between August 1972 and January 1973.[2]

Family heads in the London area communities of Slough and Wandsworth, there as the result of expulsion by Amin, reported to our interviewers.[3] Both male and female family heads were included in the study, though the vast majority of interviewees were male. In all, 77 people were surveyed in Wandsworth; 65 of these were men, and 12 were women. Slough had a much smaller recently arrived Ugandan Asian population; a dozen people were interviewed of whom only one was female. Tabulating spouses and offspring, these persons represented directly, and reported for over 450 people from both communities. No person refused to be interviewed, and to our knowledge, no head-of-household in either of these communities was overlooked by the survey.

Careful selection of communities is essential to structuring representativeness in such a study. Consultation with knowledgeable persons, and consideration of community characteristics regarded as significant to this study, resulted in the choice of Wandsworth, an inner London borough, and Slough, a population centre just west of the official Greater London boundaries. 300,000 people live in Wandsworth while Slough has 95,000 residents. Knowledgeable opinions and statistical evidence lend credence to the assumption that the ample populations are not composed of any isolated socioeconomic class or social category of people. Interviewees, collectively, can be expected to reflect attitudes, opinions and social characteristics of Ugandan Asians in general.

Social Background Characteristics

Particularly important to a population's assimilation or absorption are the traits, knowledge and lifeways they bring with them to the new society. Those British factions attempting to smooth the way for rapid

99

adjustment of the Ugandan Asians portrayed the immigrants in a manner perceived as acceptable to the dominant, native populace. 'Middle class' was a label frequently applied to the Asians; they were not, pro-Asian sectors contended, the illiterate or unskilled refugees that some earlier migrant waves had brought to the British Isles. How accurate were the preconceptions? The interviews shed some light on this question.

The level and desirability of productive skills a new population offers is of crucial importance to social absorption. The more valuable the migrant's abilities to the economy of the host nation, the more readily he will be accepted and permitted to participate in this major social institution. In many, if not most instances, the process of social absorption for males is initiated in the economic institution. Their participation is generally requisite to maintaining themselves and their families, and thus employment is immediately and intensely pursued.

True to the reported history of the Asians in Africa, as well as to the expectation of the Britishers, the vast majority of the Ugandan males had been employed in managerial positions associated with commercial establishments in their homeland — 69 per cent of the males indicated such employment. Of the remaining respondents, 22 per cent were employed in white-collar occupations, 5 per cent were professionals, and 4 per cent were skilled workers.[4] None reported having held unskilled jobs.[5]

A check at the Tooting Bec employment exchange — the Wandsworth exchange serving most of the borough's Ugandan Asians — produced the supporting data that 60 per cent of the Ugandan Asian males on the register were applicants for either white-collar or managerial-professional positions. One new arrival reported confidently to a journalist, 'I could be an asset. I have experience as an accountant. I know the travel business. I could manage any kind of small shop. I could be an asset to a company.'[6] The words could have been spoken by any number of men seeking work.

The exchange also provided some interesting and contrasting data on women seeking employment. The Asian females, far fewer of course than male applicants, were concentrated in the unskilled category. These aspirations and skill levels are one reflection of the strongly reinforced traditional role for Asian women. It was the first time many of the women, including several hoping for white-collar jobs, had sought employment outside the home. Too, their style of life in Uganda, isolated from the larger community, made knowledge of English largely unnecessary. Estimates at the national level were that 20 out of every 100 household heads in the arriving population could not speak English. The local exchange maintained that this rate was holding true for males, but that less than half of the females spoke the language. The necessary early economic involvement in the larger society offers theoretical support to the assumption that males assimilate or are absorbed into a new society more quickly than are females. It is not uncommon, given traditional family structures, for women to remain isolated from all but a segregated, homogeneous minority or migrant community for long periods of time, and in some instances, for a lifetime.

The occupational profile of the Ugandan Asian males indicates that they are skilled and accustomed to employment in the middle and upper ranks of the occupational hierarchy. As a group, their skill levels are high, and collectively, their talents should mesh well with the British economy. Problems, however, are implied by this data as well. If previous employment and positions are indicators, many of the Ugandans would logically aspire to own small businesses. While this is a reasonable aspiration in Great Britain, the problem of cash available to the immigrants for initial investments in such an endeavour is limited or inaccessible (if, for example, money is impounded in Ugandan banks). Consider, for instance, the case of a proprietor of a 'motor spares' store in Uganda, now living in London. He has willingly sought related work; yet, he does not have the technical know-how to repair or instal motor parts, and he is financially unable to purchase his own auto parts business. Opportunities for managing someone else's business are not in the offering. What does he do?

Likewise, an immigrant group with above-average skills can generate resentment on the part of natives threatened by employment competition. Some evidence anticipates that fear of competition may have sparked hostility in Britain. One such indication is the fact that, in response to a survey conducted by the Opinion Research Centre in early 1973, 60 per cent of the middle-class respondents agreed with Great Britain's policy of admitting the Ugandan Asians, while 66 per cent of those from the working class opposed the measure.[7] Those of less secure status are typically more anxious about competition, or the threat of competition than are those who are more securely established socially. A Community Relations Officer in an inner London borough reported incidents reflecting similar anxiety. Two engineering companies had mailed petitions to his office suggesting that he not try to place Asians with them; their employees did not want to work with them.[8] Prejudice and discrimination stemming from such attitudes would hamper the migrants' adaptation.

Too, in terms of absorption, educational qualifications are an important appendage to previous economic status. Lacking educational attainment, or degrees considered by the dominant society essential to holding given posts, one may discover that in spite of extensive previous experience, he is declared formally unqualified for a familiar position. Educational status is almost always difficult to compare across societies.

All nations, and even regions within nations, have managed to create educational systems which differ in some degree or another from most, if not all, others. Such developments are the result of time, tradition and probably accident, but they are significant developments nevertheless. While specific degree or examination attainments are not as relevant to general social absorption as are educational correlates such as literacy, they are often important in gaining access to specific bureaucratically organised activities.

During the last decade, the structure of the Ugandan educational system has undergone a series of reforms. Variations in labels attached to levels of schooling as a result of these changes, and as a consequence of some respondents being educated in India, posed problems for recording educational attainment. It was possible, however, in most instances where such difficulties arose to communicate in terms of educational equivalencies, or to transpose rank in one system to rank in another. The following categories were identifiable to most of the population and provided direct data comparisons with the British educational system: (1) primary school, a category comparable to the American six primary grades; (2) junior secondary school, a two-year certificate grading programme similar in many respects to the American junior high school; (3) senior secondary school, serving functions similar to that of an American high school (it consists of an initial two-year course leading to an exam to select candidates continuing toward university entrance); and (4) university and graduate school education.[9]

The typical Asian male responding to the survey had obtained a junior secondary school certificate; i.e. he had completed approximately eight years of formal education (35 per cent). However, a very similar proportion (28 per cent) of the men reported having graduated from senior secondary school. Eight per cent of the respondents had undergraduate degrees, 3 per cent had completed graduate training of one type or another, and 11 per cent had no formal education. The figures affirm the image of the educated African Asian. Educated well beyond the level of simple literacy, his scholastic attainments should promote his acceptance in a new society.[10]

Also of importance in considering educational attainment among the Asians is the fact that after the first four years of Ugandan primary education, the medium of classroom instruction is English.[11] From this, one can infer that many of the Asian male immigrants are acquainted with, and a high proportion well versed in, the English language.[12]

Additionally, and as noted, correspondence between education and occupation should be considered with a view to formal educational requisites for employment. It is apparent from our data that while many of the interviewees occupied the more prestigious positions in

Uganda, the educational achievement of those same persons tend to more nearly approximate an average or basic education in Britain. The point is not that the Asians are poorly educated; they are without doubt more highly educated than have been most other immigrant groups to Britain. It is, however, anticipated that because of lower levels of formal education, the Asians may, in many cases, not be able to satisfactorily compete for positions comparable to those they held in Uganda. Supporting this possibility, Derek Humphry and Michael Ward reported that professional and commercial leaders remained a significant group among Asians still unemployed in June 1973. Qualifications of those people were, they stated, not readily accepted by employers in Britain.[13] In simple terms of employment/unemployment, as opposed to obtaining a specific desired position, level of education may, however, be an important factor. Interviews with all nonretired Wandsworth Asian males reveal that 91 per cent of those with no formal schooling or primary education were unemployed, while 60 per cent of those with junior or senior secondary certificates were working in January 1973. Observers of the situation offer the impression that the Kenyan Asians, who came to Great Britain in large numbers in 1968, and whose social characteristics closely parallel those of the Ugandan Asians, have taken less prestigious positions than those in which they were employed in Africa.[14] An example of alleged educational deficiency which has served to prevent the immigrants from reassuming their professional roles in Great Britain is found in the case of Asian school teachers. Frequently they are required to undertake additional training in order to be invited into the British classrooms. Reported in the *Guardian* was one individual's experience, an experience not unlike many others cited in British Asian communities. The newspaper states: 'A . . . recent arrival from Kenya, a head of a school department who taught maths and English clears frames on a mill night shift. The school master has been accepted for a teaching diploma course in Manchester and in a year should be back at the blackboard.'[15]

Fear of widespread unemployment among the Asians, due to the inaccessibility of desirable jobs, is probably unwarranted. The East African Asians have shown themselves ready to work at most tasks made available to them. As one Kenyan Asian stated, '. . . you must have things hard now if you want them soft later. I know at least 130 East African families here in Oldham and only 3 of them are on unemployment benefit. . . . We have to work and the Ugandan Asians will be the same.'[16] And a resettlement centre director observed: 'We get two, three jobs a day offered — mill operator, porter, refuse collector, midwife, secretary, salesman. They're eager to take jobs, especially the young ones. There's an intense desire to start a new life. Every week that goes by, the ones that don't get jobs become more anxious about not being able to start.'[17]

The content of cultural learning, attitudes toward work as one example, is of great importance to absorption. The more closely previous learning resembles the knowledge of a receiving society, the more rapidly the integration process can take place. The obvious cultural differences between East Africa and Britain will often create serious problems for the newly arrived Asians, but often, too, amusing confrontations between the cultures will arise. One such instance occurred at West Malling camp and was recorded in the January 27, 1973 edition of *The Guardian*.

> Just coincidence – it could hardly be anything else – that Burns Night should fall on the second anniversary of the coming of Idi Amin in Uganda. But it added a certain piquancy to Burns Night at the Uganda Resettlement Board's camp at West Malling.
> Few of West Malling's 700 Asians had ever heard of Robbie Burns, but there were a dozen or so Scots and English there who had. Burns Night was celebrated in a hall full of trestle tables with sausage rolls, vegetarian sandwiches, and bulk tea. The mysteries were opened by a markedly English-looking clergyman who gave thanks to God, hands at prayer, with the word 'Namaste,' a greeting of universal holiness.
> Two mountainous pipers then appeared, ducking to get through the double doors; the effects of bagpipes on several hundred enthusiastic but puzzled Asians can only be described in terms of cultural shock. Likewise the ceremony of the haggis itself, performed with flourish by the very Scottish deputy administrator of the Hobbs camp (now closed). He saluted the Chieftain of the Pudding Race with a ceremonial George V sword lent by the deputy administrator of West Malling. It is a bizarre enough ritual even to English eyes; the Asians were amazed.[18]

Of equal importance, though often less readily observable, are the cultural structures of social organisation. When these overlap in homeland and host society, adjustment is hastened, but when they differ and conflict, the migrant in some manner or another must appease the expectations of the receiving nation.

Relying on anthropological observations, the family is one social form that could be expected to vary between an Eastern and Western society. In Britain the most prevalent form or structure of the family is acknowledged to be nuclear; parents and their unmarried offspring constitute the typical family group. This mode of family organisation is common among the Asians, but the extended family, or a nuclear family appended by other relatives, is the traditional form apparently still common in East African Asian society. Among the eighty-nine families in this survey, over half of the migrants, or 57 per cent,

104

reported living in nuclear-style families (as indicated by relatives sharing a household) in East Africa. This data does, however, confirm that a sizable proportion of the population adhered to an extended form of family. Such a definition of family, on even the most fundamental levels of adjustment, presents problems for the Asians. Housing is a case in point. Accommodations are sufficiently difficult to find, say, in London, and the added burden of trying to house an extended family must prove frustrating, if not impossible. No doubt one result of this situation is that British housing tends to force conformity to the British nuclear pattern; extended families must split up in order to be housed comfortably. Another possible response to the housing situation, which may ultimately have a similar effect on family structure, is that the larger family may decide to move into a residence unsuited to accommodate their numbers. Tensions potentially created by such arrangements could also have erosive effects on the extended structure.[19]

The important role of the larger family network among the Asians is emphasised by the fact that nearly 70 per cent of the interviewees reported that in Uganda relatives lived near them, in the same community, and that interaction among the family households was frequent. Of those reporting relatives in the same community, a full 93 per cent reported visiting with at least some of those relatives no less than once every fortnight — every fourteen days. This, and the above data, indicate that kin organisation among the Asians in Uganda was cohesive and played a major part in defining social patterns. This same cohesion can, if retained, be predicted to provide a buffer against the trials of adjustment to a new society and culture; but on the other hand, it can be seen as a cultural trait unlikely to blend easily into British society. To the extent that the family does retain its solidarity, it is also likely to interfere with adaptation by providing a shield against exposure to British life and a barrier to acculturation.

Group cohesion is indicated as well by the fact that over half (61 per cent) of the immigrants interviewed were sharing British residences with Ugandan Asian friends or relatives. Most of the accommodations were regarded as temporary, but the fact that the immigrants turn to kin and peers for substantial assistance indicates the presence of in-group solidarity. Most of the interviewees sharing households were residing with relatives, providing further indication of the existence of strong social bonds within the extended family.

A commonly held British view of the Asian family is that it is excessively fertile. The data from our interviews does not support that opinion with regard to the Ugandan Asian family. In fact, 65 per cent of the families reported having no more than three children, and the most frequently mentioned number of offspring was one. The extended family form may create the impression that families are large, but our population, at least, does not indicate the existence of large biological families. While certain studies, as well as the evidence of census data, have shown comparatively high fertility rates among the Asians relative to the English population, it may be that the East African Asians are an exception to that pattern.[20] High levels of education and living standards are factors which generally correlate with decreasing family size. That the Ugandan Asian far outranks the typical Indian and Pakistani in these two respects lends support to the speculation that smaller families may characterise the Asians from East Africa.

Unlikely to thwart the adjustment of the Ugandan Asians to Britain is the high degree of urbanisation in their host society. In spite of the fact that Uganda is still a predominantly rural nation, the Asians themselves have been city dwellers for decades. East African social and political çonditions, as discussed in Chapter 2, have left them little alternative to an urban existence. But imposed patterns of settlement do not appear to have unduly hampered the Asians' progress in East Africa; the Asians acquired marketable urban skills, and they prospered. Those talents should be readily transferable to industrial and highly urbanised Great Britain.

Fifty-three per cent of the newly arrived Asians interviewed were formerly residents of Kampala, a city of some 300,000 residents. An additional 15 per cent lived in Jinja, which has a population of 100,000. Granted, of course, that the population and size of Greater London is far larger than the capital of Uganda, that nation's largest population centre, urban life patterns are familiar to the Asians, and their previous urban residence can only enhance their adjustment in Britain.

The knowledge that the Asians resided in Uganda for decades, even for generations, raises an additional issue regarding adjustment to a new society. To what extent, and with what intensity, did the Ugandan Asians identify with the nation they had been forced to leave? To what extent did they view themselves as part of the Ugandan nation?

Strong attachment to a home and nation can, of course, inhibit adjustment to a new society. One of Amin's indicators of national loyalty – citizenship – probably does partially reflect such attachment. It is acknowledged that many Ugandan Asians did not, for whatever reasons, take advantage of the offers of Ugandan citizenship. It is also obvious that the Asians clung tenaciously to Indian lifeways and generally scorned things African. In spite of this, there is some information obtained from the interviewed group that would infer identification with the East African nation. Nearly half of that population (49 per cent), for example, were born in Uganda, and an additional 6 per cent were born elsewhere in East Africa. (With the exception of the 2 per cent who were natives of Pakistan, the remaining

106

respondents were all born in India.) Forty-two per cent of the interviewees reported that they had spent their entire lives in Uganda. It is difficult to imagine living such significant segments of one's life in a country and not developing strong attachments to it. Granted that the Asians' ties may have been first to a subculture within the larger society, nevertheless, societal identification is almost certainly intrinsic to those bonds. The degree of allegiance to, and identification with, Uganda will in part determine the Asians' ease of adjustment to Britain — the greater the level of previous identification, the more difficult the adjustment will be.

Views of Britain

As of January 1973, most of the refugees who had initially been housed in resettlement camps were at least temporarily settled in British communities.[21] Many others, of course, had never resided in the camps, but on arrival, they had joined relatives or friends already in Britain. Individual reactions and responses to the new society, of course, varied, but interesting patterns are also evident. At the time of the interviews, none of the respondents had been in Britain longer than six months, and most had been there for much shorter lengths of time. The average length of residence was three months. The respondents' views provide insights into how, during the first weeks of settlement, a group of forced immigrants perceives a new homeland and embarks on the process of adapting to it.

Early opinions of life in Great Britain tended to be favourable. Asked if they were satisfied with life in the London area, over 70 per cent of the respondents answered positively, the distribution being nearly identical for Wandsworth and Slough. Similarly, when queried as to whether they believed Great Britain would be a good place for them to spend their life, nearly three-quarters of those surveyed stated 'yes.' Obviously, some of the acceptance may be attributed to relief from having escaped the harrowing situation in East Africa, or to an unwillingness to appear ungrateful; but as nearly a quarter of the Asians expressed at least some disappointment or reservations, it is probably safe to assume that most were, in fact, content with immediate personal circumstances in Britain.

It might, however, be suggested that reported initial satisfaction is in part a product of limited interaction with the larger society. At the time they were interviewed, most of the Asians had not had extended contact with British society or its people; their residence in Britain had, in almost all cases, been spent in Asian enclaves — resettlement camps or British-Indian communities. Only half of the men were employed and exposed to the greater community in that manner. Eighty-five per

107

cent of the respondents counted no English natives among their friends; most stated that those contacts they did have with the English were formal, e.g. shopkeeper-customer relations.[22] Probably even more revealing in terms of a lack of familiarity with Britain and its lifeways, is this: While most of the Ugandan Asians, when asked, did not note British customs difficult for them to adjust to, many did state that they had not had sufficient exposure to British life to be able to make observations regarding those customs.[23] It may be hypothesised that some of the satisfaction voiced in the early stages of adaptation may be a function of not yet having reached a point at which one regularly confronts the major institutions of the society, or frequently interacts with representatives of the host society. It is not until such interaction takes place that one is required to exhibit conforming behaviour; logically, that is the time when many difficulties inherent in adapting to a new society surface.

But the immigrants did not, in this early isolation, solely convey optimism about the circumstances they faced. Slightly more than half of them believed that Englishmen are prejudiced against Asians — and/ or that Asians are discriminated against in Britain. This belief, clearly, could have been cultivated in East Africa where the Asians were long acquainted with British colonials. If not acquired there, however, the opportunities were many for acquiring a taste of British hostility in the United Kingdom itself. One Asian returned to the Tonfanau Resettlement Centre after a visit to a nearby community and questioned a volunteer worker, 'Please, what exactly is a wog?'[24] Many other Asians were to see the derogatory reference all too often sprayed on walls, scrawled in the subway and carried on pickets' placards. It would be particularly interesting to note to what degree the opinion of anti-Asian prejudice is reaffirmed after additional months' residence in Great Britain, after more extensive contact with Britishers and British society.

Health and Disposition

An aggressive Asian shoe salesman in Kampala reportedly commanded a handsome profit in August 1972 by advertising his goods as valuable apparel essential to withstanding the harsh British winter.[25] No one would deny that climates in East Africa and Britain are radically different. In spite of this change in temporal conditions, however, the great majority of the Ugandan Asians stated that they had experienced no significant changes in health since arriving in Europe. Likewise, nearly all reported that the health of their families had not been impaired by the move.

Many respondents have taken advantage of services offered them by the British Government. Among all interviewees, 84 per cent reported

108

that the health of their families had not been impaired by the move.

Many respondents have taken advantage of services offered them by the British Government. Among all interviewees, 84 per cent reported utilising the assistance of official local and/or national agencies. Some complaints were voiced, most of them dealing with the need for more concerted efforts at providing housing, employment and loans. Several respondents desired financial assistance in setting up small businesses. Another request to the Government, that stateless family members being detained in camps in Europe be permitted to join their families in Britain, was granted shortly after the interviews were taken.[26]

A psychological trait often said to characterise migrants is anomie. It infers alienation or a lack of integration into intimate social groups, community and/or larger society. It would be predictable that, while anomie is a common attribute of migrants in general, it would be even more likely to appear in a forced migrant population.

Srole's five item inventory of questions[27] was used to assess the existence of this trait among the Ugandan Asians. The items are the following: (1) 'In spite of what some people say, the lot of the average man is getting worse, not better'; (2) 'Nowadays, a person has to live pretty much for today and let tomorrow take care of itself'; (3) 'It's hardly fair to bring children into the world with the way things look for the future'; and (4) 'There's little use in writing to public officials because often they aren't really interested in the problems of the average man.'

Tabulated so that a total of five was high and zero low, the data show a clear concentration of high scores. One-third of the respondents had scores of four; 73 per cent of the respondents had scores of three, four or five. Based on Srole's scale, the Asians reveal definite anomie tendencies. While it is logical to assume that these reactions are at least in part due to the traumatic experiences they had recently encountered, it is, of course, impossible to say that those events are the specific cause of this orientation. Again, it would be valuable to seek the same information from the population at a later point in time; supposedly, they would then be better adjusted to the new society and could be expected to reveal more positive social and psychological orientations.

To anticipate optimism in the Ugandan Asian community during those first months in Britain would be unrealistic. Less than a year prior to the initiation of this investigation, many of the interviewees were involved in overseeing their own businesses; when interviewed, they were employees of others or were unemployed. Families were temporarily housed, and almost all of the Asians were dependent upon some form or another of assistance in order to maintain themselves and to structure their future in Great Britain. Most had been divested of certain social roles. Many immigrants, for example, had no Ugandan

Asian friends residing in the neighbourhood. Unemployment had created a vacuum in the occupational role. Participation in secondary groups was minimal. In many communities of settlement there were, for example, no religious facilities for certain groups. When families, both extended and nuclear, were separated, kin roles too were reduced. Yet, 82 per cent of those interviewed claimed that they would not return to Uganda even if policies and practices detrimental to Asians changed. Over 60 per cent contended that they viewed Great Britain as their home.

Prospects for Absorption

The Ugandan Asians, like immigrant groups before them, have begun the long and frequently difficult process of adjusting to life in a new country. They carry the added burden of having migrated not by choice, but by decree. Their homes, businesses and communities, a carefully cultivated and generally comfortable way of life, were left behind when the jets departed Entebbe Airport. In all probability, few will ever set foot in Uganda again.

In spite of the trauma surrounding the exodus and resettlement, the Asians appear to be making efforts toward a positive social transition. The impression is that, in terms of the stages of acceptance, acculturation and absorption, the group is well advanced into the first phase of the cycle. Especially considering the conditions of their migration, the Asians display a notable tolerance for their new surroundings and circumstances. But this ready acceptance is not necessarily an indication that the entire adaptation process will progress with ease for the Ugandans. If previous observations regarding migrant adjustment hold for this group, features characterising the immigrants and the influx may make acculturation and absorption more difficult to attain.

Among characteristics which inhibit group absorption, racial differences between host and migrant populations have been noted. While labelled by the physical anthropologists as 'Caucasian' the Indian nevertheless displays physical features which readily distinguish him from the Anglo-Saxon native of the British Isles. His appearance constitutes an unalterable barrier to easy and voluntary assimilation, to that social invisibility requisite to absorption into the larger society. The Ugandan Asians are candidates for long-standing minority status. They are identifiable to those who may wish to exclude them from full participation in society and to those who may wish to employ discriminatory methods in their dealings with the Asians.

Culturally, too, the Asians are readily distinguishable from the British population, and there are strong indications that those cultural differences are encouraged and reinforced within the British Asian communities. The reluctance to depart from the Indian lifestyle is not attributed to ignorance of British customs and ways. The East African Asians were exposed to British manners during the long colonial periods in India and Africa. In spite of the marked social distance maintained by the British between themselves and the natives of India, an Asian acquaintance with British culture must have been one product of the cohabitation. As a result of this socialisation, Asian males at least should be sufficiently sophisticated to partake easily in formal and informal social exchanges with the British in the United Kingdom. The impression, rather, is that the Asian prefers his bicultural life and strives to retain Eastern customs in most of his primary group relationships.

Adhering to cultural patterns different from those of the larger society, the Asian will continue to maintain his visibility. This need not, however, necessarily deter the Asians' eventual absorption. Pluralism has been proven a viable minority policy in several nations. The Asians themselves indicated a preference for pluralism in Africa; that pluralism, however, bordered on isolation from the larger society and was characterised by a failure to participate fully in all facets, notably politics, of that society. This isolation, reinforced by the British colonials and later reaffirmed by ignoring opportunities to assimilate into African society, contributed to the Asians' later demise under the independent regime. The Asians' previous experience in a multicultural society may induce them to operate with a more open definition of their role in British society. If so, a role definition with less emphasis on social segregation may surface in Britain. For the time being, the Asians seem content with a culturally marginal position in British society. Whatever the Ugandan Asians may choose, it is apparent that the vast majority, in order to adapt to the new society, will acquire a greater knowledge and acceptance of British lifeways.

Size and rapidity of population influx also may affect adaptation of migrant groups. Theoretically the size of the Ugandan Asian migration should not be detrimental to their adjustment. There is a steady flow of immigrants into Britain. In 1971 nearly 200,000 of them entered the country. Seen in this perspective, the 28,000 Ugandan Asians represent only a fraction of the normal immigration. However, almost all of them arrived during a seven-week period, and the concentrated nature of the influx heightened the impact of the relatively modest size of the migration. This factor, plus earlier gross overestimates of the number of the incoming deportees, produced what seemed an equally exaggerated reaction in Britain.

It must be acknowledged that the backlash resulting from news of the Asians' arrival was due, in part, to essentially racial prejudices against New Commonwealth immigrants. Not only did the forced exit of the Ugandan Asians distress those who would protect Britain from

111

nonwhite immigration, but also distressing were the additional tens of thousands of British Asians (75,000 in East Africa alone) vulnerable to a similar fate. In response to such a possibility, Her Majesty's Government announced it no longer would tolerate threats of mass expulsion. Britain's commitments to its East African Asian passport holders would be honoured, but only if their entry into the United Kingdom would take place within the quotas established under terms of recent Immigration Acts. 'What type of passport is it which refuses to protect a man when he needs it?' the *Guardian* asked in its February 3 weekly edition. The price necessary for the United Kingdom to pay to keep out a few thousand British Asians seemed high — a tarnishing of a proud tradition of legality and humanity. Its willingness to pay that price reflected the uneasiness the British people were feeling toward coloured immigration.

The basic mood in Britain as the Ugandan Asians arrived was clearly a hostile one. Yet the Government, assisted by concerned voluntary organisations and private citizens, organised reception procedures to a degree far greater than had ever been done before. The formal as well as informal reception accorded the Ugandan Asians by the British is destined to intervene in the absorption process. The Government and the Uganda Resettlement Board played the major roles during the early months of what might be described as Phase I, or the relocation stage, in the absorption of the refugee population. What did they accomplish in these first dramatic months? Their business, the URB argued, was to receive the arrivals and to relocate them in Britain. Results of these activities were solid ones. The processing for emigration of close to 30,000 British Asians in Uganda, their subsequent removal to Britain, their reception at, and funnelling through, airports to relatives, friends, other countries or resettlement centres, and the relocation by April of 80 per cent of the almost 22,000 who had gone to the centres — these were impressive achievements. Resettlement, as opposed to relocation of the Asians, was to be quite a different matter.

Evidence mounts that the problems of many Ugandan Asian families are not being alleviated. Critics argue that it was absurd to attempt to treat the Ugandan Asians like any other citizens once they were resident in British communities. It is true that even among immigrants, they are a special group. Most came devoid of financial resources of any kind. Many arrived with family members separated by distance and government fiat. Some had no desire whatsoever to be in Britain.

The argument behind establishing a statutory body to deal with Ugandan Asians was in fact a recognition of the special character of these refugees. Yet the Government placed severe limitations on the Board's powers. It decided that once the Asians were relocated by whatever process, they no longer were the Board's responsibility. And

112

then, as an unfortunate exclamation point to those decisions, the Government included 'resettlement' in the Board's name.

The final responsibility for permanent settlement of the Asians was to be on the Asians' own shoulders. Whatever assistance they received would be that which the often hard-pressed local agencies could provide. As the Board was moving toward a resolution of its formal obligations and toward its own likely dissolution, the actual resettlement process was just getting under way.

In terms of adaptation, the Ugandan Asians provided evidence during the first year of settlement of a willingness to secure available initial employment at unskilled levels and then to begin the arduous task of matching skills with opportunities where suitable housing was available. For some, occupational emergence in British society will take less than a year; for others, the process may take several years. Many will probably never achieve positions comparable in prestige and income to those they held in East Africa. All will, at least, be laying the groundwork for the anticipated economic success of their offspring.

The fate of the Asian women is far more difficult to predict. For most, their traditional roles will no doubt dictate limited access to British society and consequently retard, or even prevent, absorption into the larger society. Adaptation will be focused more narrowly on neighbourhood, community and subculture. But for others the upheaval in Ugandan Asian society caused by crisis migration may stimulate changes in personal life styles; it may generate a re-examination of their social role and identity. The fact that the adjustment of female migrants, half of the world's migrant population, has been so completely neglected by researchers is a distressing and deplorable discovery. It is one further reason for urging continuation of this and related research.

Evidence available in Wandsworth and Slough during the first year lends credence to the belief that the goals and expectations of the Ugandan Asians are such that they will *not* be satisfied with dilapidated housing, substandard living conditions, underemployment and lower socioeconomic neighbourhoods. As the family begins to shape its position in its new homeland, considerable shifts in employment and housing are likely. How soon these new immigrants will begin to depend less on the security of living near their predecessors in dominant Asian neighbourhoods and begin instead to seek the middle-class neighbourhoods to which they and other Asians aspire, will depend partly upon the loans and deposits allowed by public authorities and private associations (including, importantly, the Asian organisations). The potential for dispersal of the Ugandan Asians across, for example, Greater London, among the middle-class neighbourhoods is great, if financial and housing policies are amended or interpreted to encourage this distribution. Housing discrimination must, of course, also be circumvented. Their dispersal will also depend to a great extent upon social and cultural orientations to the new society: will Ugandan Asians prefer cultural pluralism and the consequent benefits of some isolation from the larger community? Or will they opt for assimilation and as much interaction with the larger society as the dominant group will allow? Regardless of conditions they confront or decisions they make, the major portion of the resettlement process, whether in terms of employment, housing or other requisites for establishing oneself and one's family, will most likely be initiated and pursued by the immigrants themselves.

The dominant community relations approach encourages all parties — whether they be new or old residents, rich or poor, coloured or white, educated or uneducated — to recognise that the sure way to acceptance by the majority is to pursue behaviour patterns conducive to gradual adaptation to the prevailing lifestyle. The problem is that this approach does not distinguish among types of potential 'adapters.' Rarely do policymakers take into consideration the various forms of immigration and types of immigrants. Conditions of in-migration vary considerably among individuals and groups; these differences will require variation in form and duration of response by the host society. Not the least of the factors that will affect the Ugandan Asians' adaptation to Britain is the form of migration that brought them to the British Isles. Forced migrants can be expected to make societal transitions more slowly than will those who carefully plan and anticipate movements to a new nation.

An understanding of the initial adaptation process as it relates to the Ugandan Asians in Britain is valuable, in and of itself; but the phenomenon of forced migration is worthy of careful attention in a longitudinal manner. It would be possible to analyse the social characteristics and reactions of the migrant population over a period of years. Governmental response, population dispersal, spatial mobility and settlement, also are best examined in the perspective of time. Before the Ugandan Asians lose their identity amidst the thousands of Indians and Pakistanis in Britain, as they inevitably will do, concerted efforts should be made to record their progress along the way to absorption. Such knowledge would prove invaluable to nations and officials called upon to deal with the phenomenon of forced migration. On a larger scale, such research enriches the understanding of human conditions and responses in a socially and politically troubled world.

Notes

1. Heads-of-households or family heads were defined as married persons living with spouse and/or children. To our knowledge, this definition did not

114

exclude from the sample any person whose spouse was stateless. In these cases, the spouse in Britain had a child or children of that marriage in his or her care.

2. This sampling strategy, i.e. surveying all persons with specific characteristics who reside in designated geographic areas, or 'total populations,' permits generalisation from the base to the larger aggregate. The unit about which one wishes to generalise in this instance is all expelled Ugandan Asian household heads in Britain. The researcher whose budget prohibits a systematic sampling of all representatives of the phenomenon under study aspires to include a valid cross-section of that group by alternatively interviewing all representatives resident in carefully selected geographic areas.

3. This settlement may be in many cases only temporary. In the process of compiling rolls of the Ugandan Asian population in these communities, it quickly became evident that several families who had initially settled in Wandsworth or Slough had moved to other locations in Great Britain. (Reports on these moves left the impression that they were frequently within the Greater London area.) The fact that a large proportion of these people (90 per cent) regard their housing as temporary, indicates that some physical mobility, some of which will no doubt be intercommunal, must be anticipated.

4. Unless otherwise noted, all tabulations are based on responses from both Wandsworth and Slough populations.

5. Two of the thirteen women interviewed had been employed in Uganda; both had been white-collar workers. Given the fact that head-of-household status is an unlikely status for the Ugandan Asian women, it would be inappropriate to generalise from this small and atypical population to all women. While, given the structure and organisation of the Asian family, it is a reasonable assumption that few women were employed, it would be necessary to survey all women, not just heads-of-households, in order to defend or refute that assumption.

6. Bernard Weinraub, 'Starting all Over,' *New York Times*, December 24, 1972.

7. Reported in 'Immigrants,' *New Society*, March 8, 1973, p. 536.

8. Weinraub, *op. cit.*, p. 11.

9. For a description of education in Uganda, see Martena Sasnett and Inez Sepmeyer, *Educational Systems of Africa* (Berkeley, 1966), pp. 325-329.

10. It is interesting to note that gamma, a statistical measure of association between variables, is very high between sex and level of education for this population. Here, being male is associated with high educational attainment, and being female is associated with low educational attainment. A perfect relationship between these variables as measured by gamma in the direction described would be 1·00; in this instance, G = 0·91. Again, however, it is unfair to generalise from the small number of female family heads to all Asian women. Although it may be the case, one cannot infer that most Ugandan Asian women, as compared with men, have attained little education. The suggestion does, however, prompt further speculation about varying rates of societal adaptation between the sexes. Education is recognised as important to absorption, and if men are more highly educated, they will be absorbed more rapidly.

11. Sasnett and Sepmeyer, *op.cit.,* p. 327

12. Other information sources confirm, however, that the language situation is not ideal. According to Department of Employment statistics, of five thousand Asians who were unemployed and seeking jobs in the spring of

1973, over one thousand required training in fundamentals of the English language in order to obtain a position. (Reported in Derek Humphry and Michael Ward, 'Promises,' *The Sunday Times*, June 10, 1973.) The group is, of course, not a cross-section of the immigrant population, and one may assume that among the employed, the vast majority were familiar with the language of the land. Nevertheless, communication is without doubt a problem for a segment of the Ugandan Asians.

13. Derek Humphry and Michael Ward, 'Promises,' *The Sunday Times,* June 10, 1973.
14. See, for example, Alan Little and Josephine Toynbee, 'The Asians: A Threat or an Asset?' *New Society*, October 26, 1972, p. 206.
15. Gillian Linscott, 'Asians Will Go Through the Mill,' *The Guardian*, September 16, 1972.
16. *Ibid.*, p. 9.
17. Weinraub, *op. cit.*, p. 12.
18. 'Miscellany.'
19. In this context, it is interesting to note one of the consistent observations of social service personnel regarding problems of initial housing among the newly arrived Asians. Refugees moving in with relatives would at first be well received, but following a time span of a few weeks, the overcrowding and its consequent pressures commonly produced disharmony in the family group. Such rifts were frequently cited in justifying requests for additonal housing.
20. Research carried out in Sparkbrook, Birmingham by Rex and Moore for example, reports the average number of live births for women ever pregnant for Asians to be 4·0 and for the English to be 2·7. See J. Rex and R. Moore, *Race and Community Conflict: A Study of Sparkbrook* (London, 1967).
21. The Resettlement Board's 'Analysing Operational Position,' January 1, 1973, reported that of the 21,281 Ugandans who had entered camps in 1972, 13,582 had departed.
22. Not surprisingly, very few of the interviewees reported contact of any kind with the West Indian population. Patterns of racial segregation, both physical and social, are readily observable and acknowledged. Rigidity of the patterns is comparable in intensity to Black-White segregation in the United States.
23. Among the relatively few features of British life that were noted as difficult to adjust to were food, language and the 'reserved manner' of the British.
24. David Blundy, *The Sunday Times*, November 12, 1972.
25. *Sunday Times Magazine*, December 24, 1972.
26. The decision was announced by Home Secretary Robert Carr on February 22, 1973.
27. For an elaboration of items and a discussion of their relationship to anomie, see Leo Srole, 'Social Integration and Certain Corollaries: An Exploratory Study,' *American Sociological Review*, 216 (December 1956), pp. 706-716.

SELECTED BIBLIOGRAPHY

Allen, Sheila, *New Minorities, Old Conflicts: Asian and West Indian Migrants in Britain,* New York, 1971.

Andrews, Charles Freer, *The Indian Question in East Africa,* Nairobi, 1921.

1971 Annual Abstract of Greater London Statistics, Greater London Council.

Banton, Michael, *Racial Minorities,* London, 1972.

Bharati, Agehananda, *The Asians in East Africa: Jayhind and Ûhuru,* Chicago, 1972.

Bolitho, Hector (ed.), *The British Empire,* London, 1948.

Burney, Elizabeth, *Housing on Trial: A Study of Immigrants and Local Government,* London, 1967.

1971 Census, Great Britain, Advance Analysis. London, 1972.

Community Relations Council, *One Year On: A Report on the Resettlement of the Refugees from Uganda in Britain,* London, 1974.

Coupland, Sir Reginald, *The Exploitation of East Africa,* London, 1968.

Cross, Colin, *The Fall of the British Empire, 1918-1968,* London, 1968.

Deakin, Nicholas, *Colour, Citizenship and British Society,* London, 1970 1970.

Delf, George, *Asians in East Africa,* London, 1962.

Eisenstadt, S.N., *The Absorption of Immigrants,* London, 1952.

Eliot, Sir Charles, *East African Protectorate,* London, 1905.

Field, Frank, and Harkin, Patricia, *Black Britons,* London, 1971.

Foley, Donald L., *Governing the London Region,* Berkeley, 1972.

Ghai, Dharam, and Ghai, Yash (eds), *Portrait of a Minority,* Nairobi, 1970.

Graham, Gerald Sandford, *A Concise History of the British Empire,* New York, 1970.

Gregory, Robert D., *India and East Africa,* London, 1971.

Harlow, Vincent, Chilver, E.M., and Smith, Allison (eds), *The History of East Africa,* II, London, 1965.

Hill, Michael J., and Issacharoff, Ruth M., *Community Action and Race Relations,* London, 1971.

Hollingsworth, Lawrence W., *The Asians of East Africa,* New York, 1960.

Humphry, Derek, and Ward, Michael, *Passports and Politics,* London, 1974.

Ingham, Kenneth, *A History of East Africa,* New York, 1965.

Johnston, Sir Harry Hamilton, *The Uganda Protectorate,* London, 1902.

Knaplund, Paul, *The British Empire, 1815-1939,* New York, 1941.

Krausz, Ernest, *Ethnic Minorities in Britain,* London, 1972.

Kuper, Hilda, *Indian People in Natal,* Durban, 1960.

Mangat, J.S., *A History of the Asians in East Africa,* London, 1969.

Miller, Charles, *The Lunatic Express,* New York, 1971.

Morris, H.S., *The Indians in Uganda,* Chicago, 1968.

Oliver, Roland Anthony, *Sir Harry Johnston and the Scramble for Africa,* London, 1957.

Patterson, Sheila, *Immigrants in Industry,* London, 1968.

_____, *Immigration and Race Relations in Britain, 1960-1967,* London, 1969.

Plender, Richard, 'The Expulsion of the Asians from Uganda; Legal Aspects,' *New Community*, I, No. 5, Autumn, 1972.

Rex, J. and Moore, R., *Race and Community Conflict: A Study of Sparkbrook,* London, 1967.

Robinson, Ronald, and Gallagher, John, *Africa and the Victorians: The Official Mind of Imperialism.* London, 1961.

Rose, E.J.B., *Colour and Citizenship,* London, 1969.

Rose, J. Holland, Newton, A.P., and Benians, E.A. (eds), *The Cambridge History of the British Empire,* Cambridge, 1929.

Sasnett, Martena and Sepmeyer, Inez, *Educational Systems of Africa,* Berkeley, 1966.

Tilbe, Douglas, *The Ugandan Asian Crisis,* London, 1972.

Uganda Resettlement Board, *Final Report.* Cmnd. 5544, HMSO, London, April, 1974.

Walker, Eric Anderson, *The British Empire: Its Structures and Spirit,* 2nd edn, London, 1953.

Ward, Robin H., 'The Decision to Admit,' *New Community,* I, No. 5, Autumn, 1972.

Williamson, James Alexander, *A Short History of British Expansion,* 2 vols, London, 1964.

_____, *Great Britain and the Empire,* London, 1946.

Wright, Peter J., *The Coloured Worker in British Industry,* London, 1968.

INDEX

120